WILD ADVENTURES

FINDING JOY
IN THE JOURNEY

CAROLYN SOTO JACKSON

All Scripture quotations are from the *Holy Bible, New King James Version* © copyright 1979, 1980, 1982 by Thomas Nelson, Inc., Nashville, Tennessee. Used by permission. All rights reserved.

Original cover design by Heidi Doe.

Published by:

McDougal & Associates
18896 Greenwell Springs RD
Greenwell Springs, LA 70739
www.thepublishedword.com

McDougal & Associates is dedicated to spreading the Gospel of the Lord Jesus Christ to as many people as possible in the shortest time possible.

ISBN 978-1-950398-63-8

Printed on demand in the U.S., the U.K., Australia and the U.A.E. For Worldwide Distribution

DEDICATION

To Dan, my beloved and favorite adventurer: you truly are my everything. Thank you for always supporting my wildest dreams. Always remember, you are one of them.

To my late mother, Teresa, my daddy Joe, my stepdad, Ezequiel, and my sister Laura: thank you for a genuinely fun and loving childhood.

"But know this: when Jesus invites us on an adventure, He shapes who we become with what happens along the way."

— Bob Goff, *Love Does*[1]

1. Nashville, TN, Nelson Books: 2012

Contents

Trust in the LORD *with all your heart,*
And lean not on your own
understanding;
In all your ways acknowledge Him,
And He shall direct your paths.
— Proverbs 3:5-6

PROLOGUE

MY ADVENTURES

When was the last time you actively invited God into your daily routine? I am not talking about fasting or praying in the morning or dancing around in your socks to the song *God's Great Dance Floor*. I am talking about setting a plate for the Lord after a long day at work and inviting Him to sit with you around the table while you fling spaghetti onto your ceiling to see if it is ready or lighting a candle and intimately reciting the Song of Songs. This is the kind of invitation in which you must humble yourself in front of people in coffee shops, restaurants, or your neighbor's front door at which you have never knocked.

I invite you to join me for the next twenty-one days as I recount wild adventures I have had while encountering God. Whether these adventures included batter, paint, or sweat, God was always invited, and He always showed up. I had the humbling experience of learning to travel with a wild God, and I do not regret one single moment I have spent with my Father. My hope is this book will ignite your creativity and imagination and give you a new sense of your wondrous God.

It is up to us to invite our Father into our daily lives. He yearns for our time, our invitation, and most of all, a relationship with us.

He wants us to seek Him. He wants us to chase Him with loving eyes, grasping His presence with our bare hands. All I can say is: Do it, jump in. Jump into His grace and jump into His arms. Jump into adventures with Jesus, and do not wait!

The adventures of these next twenty-one days are only examples of the wild adventures we can all have encountering the Lord. Now is the time for you to create your own journeys and adventures with the Almighty. May you find joy in the journey!

Carolyn M. Soto Jackson
Houston, Texas

Part 1

Traveling Wild

A PILE OF DIRT

Before last summer, every time I opened my Bible to Matthew 13, I thought of wheat, tares, mustard seeds, and a whole bunch of challenging work. But this year, it made me think of a funny inside joke between my family and me while we were on a road trip through Wyoming.

We were all piled in a van gawking at the beautiful plains. About one hundred miles outside of Wyoming, we saw a large, brown historical sign which read, "Point of Interest." Later, we saw the same sign about fifty miles out and again ten miles out. By then, we were at the edge of our seats, excited to see this incredible piece of history.

One mile out, we saw the last tin sign. We began slowing down, peering out of the van, noses pressed up against the windows, and then we saw it. It was nothing but a big pile of dirt. There was absolutely nothing in or around it. It was just a pile of dirt.

We all looked at each other in disbelief. "Did we miss it?" we asked. We looked back and again, for miles, there was just land and the big pile of dirt. For more than a hundred miles, God had us on a wide-eyed and bushy-tailed adventure. In thirteen days of beautiful nature, wildlife, and mountains, I will never forget the excitement we all had leading up to the infamous, "Point of Interest," also known as a pile of dirt.

What amazes me is that when I saw this huge, dusty pile of dirt, in my spirit, I saw rich, beautiful soil. My mind later wondered what was going on underneath. What exactly was that soil for? Who was building it? What was it going to be?

All I know is someone somewhere knows there is something underneath that will eventually have many people oohing and aahing over it. Someone bought that piece of land and had begun creating something wonderful for the world to see. Someone had sown seeds below and was now in the process of watching it grow.

In Matthew 13, we read several parables, most of them about sowing good seed in good ground. There are a few things that resonate with me after reading these passages.

It is apparent to me we do not put seeds in the ground and instantly dig them up to make sure they are growing as they should. We trust what is going on underneath the soil by God's grace. We know if God has asked us to do something, we must only abide in His request. There is no need to go back every day and try to figure out what God has planned.

Another revelation I received is God encourages us to be good and fertile ground, so we can bear much fruit. If we are full of weeds, stones, and thorns, we will not be able to produce what God has called us to. We can be confident that every seed sown is being watered, nurtured, and well taken care of. All we must do is abide until the harvest.

Lastly, we must be honest, loyal, and obedient to God's Word and not be distracted by the enemy. We are encouraged to sow wheat instead of tares. Yes, they both might look the same in the beginning, but when the fruit begins to mature, it is quite apparent that the tares will eventually end up in the furnace of fire. Fortunately for us, the sons and daughters of the Most High God, we have eyes to see and ears to hear, and we know how to wholeheartedly abide, even if it takes a little more time.

A CLOSING PRAYER

Thank You, Lord, for teaching me how to be curious. Father God, teach me to be curious about You and curious about others. I ask You, Lord, to give me the heart of a child, to have faith. Let my heart reflect You always. Amen.

YOUR REFLECTIONS

1. In what ways has God drawn you nearer to Him?

2. Make your own pile of dirt. Purchase a small succulent or cactus. Carefully remove some leaves by gently twisting the leaf from the stem. Set the cuttings on a bed of soil and water for root growth over a few weeks. Plant your cuttings or give them away as gifts.

ROCKS OF REMEMBRANCE

Lake McDonald, in the heart of Montana, is known for its remarkably clear water and striking multi-colored rocks below its surface. However, when removed from the water, these vibrant rocks are no longer as red, green, or blue as they once seemed. This reminds us of the importance of being submerged in the living water of God's presence and a reminder of how God kept His promise to the children of Israel.

You may be thinking, "How?" These aged rocks were formed from clay under extreme heat and pressure caused by the glaciers. The vivid colors come from iron in their composition and the presence or absence of water. The red rocks show that oxygen was present when they were formed. The green rocks indicate they were formed in deep water, in an atmosphere lacking oxygen. Pressure and heat over many years resulted in beauty decades later. If God does this for rocks (see Matthew 6:28-30), can you imagine what He does for His children?

Just as God brought them through the Red Sea, He also guided His children as they crossed the Jordan river. While crossing, God gave Joshua instructions for twelve men to pick up twelve stones.

These twelve stones were used to construct a memorial as a reminder of God's fulfilled promise.

Similar to Aaron's breastplate (see Exodus 28:15-21), these twelve stones were a constant reminder of perseverance, deliverance, and redemption. These stones from the river allowed God's glory to shine, not only below water, but also above.

We know our obedience to God's commands enhances His Kingdom. When we obey, miracles happen, waters part, and walls come crumbling down. But it takes our steadfast love, obedience, and faithfulness while we are in the waiting, especially under the pressure and heat of the world. We can be confident in this: if we are firm in the waiting, God will create beauty, not only in Heaven, but also here on Earth.

A Closing Prayer

Father God,

Thank You for creating me out of clay, molding me into something beautiful. Thank You for the extreme heat and pressure You put me through because I know this builds character and a sensitive heart toward You and other people. I am grateful that You put me first always.

In Jesus' name,
Amen!

1. Where are you when you hear God loud and clear?

2. Go out in nature and find a smooth rock to write on. After dusting it off, write a prayer on it and place it in your garden or on your patio.

GONE FISHIN'

At three, I was handed my first fishing rod. My parents would take me out to Palestine, Texas, where we were surrounded by tall pine trees, smoky campfires, and large bodies of water. Whether I was on land with my mom or on a boat with my daddy, I was always fishing.

Years flew by as they normally do, I grew up, and things began changing within my family. One thing always remained the same: both Mom and Dad would go fishing with me.

When my husband Daniel came into my life, my first instinct was to take the city boy on one of my most beloved adventures, fishing. We packed up and headed to my daddy's place in Coldspring, Texas.

Once there, I handed Dan a pole and a box of worms. He stared back at me like I had asked him to do open heart surgery. Truth be told, he was not about to touch a slimy worm. I giggled and baited his hook for him. Then I taught him how to cast a line, watch the bobber, and then reel it in when he saw the bobber go down and felt a tug on his line.

Together we cast out our lines, and we sat and waited. Twenty minutes turned into thirty, then forty-five minutes, then an hour, and there was nothing, not a single bite. There we were, freshly dating, and now in a seriously awkward silence.

Eventually I saw Dan pull in his line and put his fishing rod aside. He was done, and we had not caught a single fish.

This reminded me of a fisherman in the Bible. He did not fish just for an hour. He fished *"all night long,"* and, like us, *"he caught nothing."* He put in the time and effort, but came up empty-handed!

I believe we all do this. We set out on a fishing adventure, and we do not realize the time, effort and cost that goes into it ... until we come up empty-handed and leave the boat.

Just like Simon, some of us are feeling disappointed or discouraged because it is costing us more than we expected when we set out on this adventure.

The story of Simon and his fishing venture is found in Luke 5. In the opening verses of the chapter, we find a frustrated fisherman who was about to have an encounter with Jesus.

Jesus was at the shoreline when He found Simon had abandoned his boat. He saw a frustrated Simon washing his nets. This is good news because it means Jesus sees you too. He also sees me. He sees us struggle and knows everything that matters to us. He knows and it also matters to Him.

Jesus sees your finances. He sees your marriage. He sees your job. Just like He saw Simon Peter that day, He sees you, and He sees me. Not one moment goes by, not one tear is shed, and not one thought is overlooked by Jesus. He cares, and He is there with us.

In verse 2, Jesus saw that the fisherman had left their boat (discouragement, disappointment) and were *"washing their nets."* Unlike Daniel, myself, or my parents, these men did not fish with rods and reels. They fished with nets. It took several men working together to throw out their enormous net which would slowly sink to the bottom, picking up algae, rocks, debris, and (hopefully) fish!

I do not know about you, but after an entire, empty night of fishing the last thing I would be doing is washing my net. To be honest, I might just throw it in the trash on my way out. But even though Simon was done fishing for that day, these men were *"tending"* their nets, getting out the debris, algae, and rocks.

Jesus never said anything negative or scolded Simon for this. The fact he was washing or tending his nets, even if he was done with them for the day, showed Simon intended to use them again. Even if he was frustrated in the moment, he planned to get back out there and try again another day.

There is nothing wrong with tending your nets. It is a time to prepare, to get your mind in the right place so you can get back to your fishing adventure. Wash your nets, just do not sell them or discard them.

When Jesus saw the boat Simon had abandoned, He immediately recognized it as a perfect platform to teach from. That boat, which represented so much despair, irritation, and angst, was to be a blessing. Jesus got into it and shared from there His message with the multitude of people that gathered on the shore.

Not only does Jesus see us, but He will also meet us in what we thought was a useless situation, and He will make it useful for His glory.

God saw Joseph when he was in prison. He saw Gideon when he was hiding in the wine press. He saw Hagar, when she had been used and abused. Oh, yes, He sees us, and He sees our abandoned boats and situations. He can and will use our abandoned boat situations for His glory.

Jesus could have easily said, "Fish, get in the boat!" and we know good and well what would have happened. But He did not. He said to Simon Peter, *"Launch out into the deep and let down your nets for a catch"* (Luke 5:4). He wanted Simon to participate with Him. And He wants that for us, as well. His desire is a relationship with us based on faith and trust.

Simon knew better than to say, "Why don't You worry about preaching, and I'll worry about fishing." He said, *"Nevertheless, at Your word, I will let down the nets"* (verse 5). In this moment, Simon trusted Jesus. He knew he was better off in deep water with Jesus than in shallow water alone.

And the same is true for us. We are better off with God's presence than in shallow water standing on our own two feet. Our feet will fail us.

If we believe our God is in control, then we must put this into effect in our daily lives when things do not go our way. If Simon had caught all those fish that night, Jesus would not have had anywhere to stand and deliver His message.

God will allow us not to have our way, to give Him a place to shine. In this way, He will create an opportunity on our behalf. If we have all our needs met without His intervention, there is no room for Him.

When we fish and we drag in the algae, rocks, and debris and still come up empty-handed, it is probably because He is about to fill our net up with something much better—Himself. At just the right moment, He will pull us out of our situation.

So, if God has been calling you to the deep waters, go! It might seem deep, risky, and scary, but if He is calling you, as He did Simon, remember what happened that day. The shallow water was to instruct the crowd of people, but the deep water was to teach Simon a lesson in faith. When we are obedient and launch out in faith, we will see an abundance of harvest in all aspect of our lives. We will see the fruit. We will see our nets breaking, full of fish.

We will see our financial situation go from indebtedness to abundance. We will see the past resentment in our families turn to forgiveness. We will see our broken marriages be restored. With Jesus, we witness the fruit of our fishing adventures.

If He is calling you back to the boat you abandoned, to the deep waters of your fishing adventure, be reckless and adventurous enough to step out in faith and meet Him.

A CLOSING PRAYER

Lord God,

I pray that we be "all in." I pray we will step out once again on this adventure You called us on. I pray You will meet us here in the deep blue sea and make us aware of Your presence. Father, I ask for another beautiful touch by You, to remind us we are never without Your presence.

In Jesus' name,
Amen!

YOUR REFLECTIONS

1. In what way is God calling you out into the deep?

2. What in your life is pushing you over the edge? Pray for God's wisdom to navigate this situation.

True North

One day a person I was talking with started the conversation by saying, "You know that one person you just hate?" I shrugged and looked over with what I know was a confused face.

When I didn't respond, they continued, "Come on, we all have that one person. You have to have one, everyone does." For several minutes they tried, in this way, to convince me that it was "normal" to hate someone at that level.

It was then that God said to me. "Not true!" I was reminded of Ezekiel 36:26, which says, *"I will give you a new heart and pour a new spirit in you; I will remove from you your heart of stone and give you a heart of flesh."* In that very moment, God gave me a revelation. Oh my, I have a new heart!

There I sat, listening to the enemy trying to convince me of something, from which I had been delivered from, but now the devil was trying to convince me I was odd because I did not agree with the individual's statement.

I continued to tell the individual to dislike someone is just not in me anymore. I hated no one, I disliked no one, and I had no enemies. To my surprise, the person was left speechless by all of this.

What the person did not know was I had been praying for three and half years for a new heart. During my very first visit to Our Fellowship Christian Church, the pastor took Daniel and me to what is now our library and asked if he could pray for me. The very first question he asked me was, "What do you want?"

My answer was, "Can I have a new heart?"

It took three and half years for me to realize God had been changing my heart the entire time.

I do not remember how the conversation ended, but I do remember God saying, "Carolyn, people are just people, and don't forget, you are one of them." None of us are sinless as Jesus was, and those of us who know Him should try to do our absolute best to be like Him.

The first eight verses of Philippians 2 teach us to think and act like Jesus, to become servants, to humble ourselves and be fully obedient to God. We must be kind to one another and walk in love. These are all attributes of being Christ-like.

Another example is found in Ephesians 4:31. In the grand scheme of things, we can narrow down our ten commandments (see Exodus 20:1-17) to two simple ones:

1. To love our God and
2. To love one another.

Seems easy, right? I do not know about you, but this is not always easy for me. It is easy to love our friends and family, but I want to know how easy it is to love your neighbor. This includes:

- The neighbor who sits across from your cubicle and smacks their gum and insists on gossiping about you in the break room.
- The neighbor who washes your windshield with dirty water and a newspaper and lets it run down on your freshly-washed vehicle.
- The neighbor who borrowed a hundred dollars, promising to pay you back "next week," but never did.
- The neighbor who cuts you off in the right-turn only lane and then turns left.

Yes, those neighbors.

The truth is: God's idea of loving our neighbor is not anywhere near our idea of loving our neighbor. Jesus loved His neighbor and even shared the Last Supper with Judas, when he had taken thirty pieces of silver as a bribe to give Jesus over to those who wanted to kill Him. Jesus loved Peter even after He knew Peter would deny Him three times. Jesus loved His neighbors by washing the feet of them all.

Those are only three examples of Jesus loving His neighbors, and there are many, many more. So, let me ask you a question. Answer in your heart. Would you invite someone over for dinner if you knew they had taken money from your enemies in exchange for giving you up to them? Would you lovingly break bread with someone you knew would deny you three times? Would you get down on your knees during a meal and wash someone's feet? Wash everyone's feet?

Our idea of loving our neighbor seems to be completely different than how Jesus loved His neighbors (even His enemies).

Those people who stab you in the back or seem difficult are a part of God's plan. Remember, Jesus could not go to the cross without a Judas.

So, how can we be more like Jesus? Engage people, all people, with love. Treat everyone you encounter as if they were Jesus. When we encounter people who rub us the wrong way, we have to put our pride in check and decide we are not trying to be right; we are trying to be like Jesus. We do not have to agree with people, but we should engage them with love nevertheless.

We have to ask ourselves, "Have I spent my whole life avoiding the people Jesus engaged?"

For instance, in traffic, avoid saying, "I am not letting that car in front of me. They should wait in line like everyone else." Instead, pray, "Lord, protect them on their drive to wherever they are traveling today."

Avoid saying, "I cannot let her get ahead of me. I am better than her, and I have been doing this much longer." Engaging, like Jesus, says, "Lord, how can I help her grow? How can I reinforce her strengths?"

Is God any less wowed if you fly across the country versus walking across the street? Not at all. We just have to encounter people with love. Whether it is in Africa or under the bridge. Whether they are nice or not so nice. Our job is not to judge people's characters or to get back at them for the way they have treated us. Our job is to love them. We must check our hearts and give people grace. Maybe they are lost or are a little turned around.

Speaking of being turned around, I know there are at least two types of people in the world:

1. People like my husband Daniel who give directions like this: "Go southbound on I-45, then exit at so and so street. Drive toward the east side of town until you arrive at the west coast of something or other.

2. Then there are people like me, who give directions like this: "Go to the second street and take a right at the stop sign. When you see a blinking light, take a left. If you see the fire station, you have gone too far and need to turn around and make a right at the blue fire hydrant.

Daniel and I think differently when it comes to directions. In fact, once he tried to teach me how to navigate without a GPS, and I about keeled over. I do not know about you, but when I was in school "north" was in front of me. In my mind, even if I turn around, North is still straight ahead. This does not mean I cannot get around; I just take a unique way of getting there. Sometimes, I get turned around, and so does Dan. But God does not because He is the True North.

Jesus did not write about loving your neighbor as a metaphor. He really wants us to love our neighbors as ourselves. Why? Because this builds our character into love. This makes us more like Him.

So, get out of your comfort zone. This will help you grow. Build relationships with people, even if it takes a bit of your time.

We must head toward True North (Jesus). Our humility with others will help us become more like Him because at the end of the day, I want to be known for my love, not my opinions of others.

CLOSING PRAYER

Lord God,

Thank You for inviting me on a brand-new adventure. Thank You for Your steadfast love, mercy, and grace while you buff out the parts of me which need to change. Thank You, Father, for teaching me how to trust more in whatever grand adventure You have for me. Thank You, Lord, for providing family and friends who support and help steer me in the right direction. I want to thank You for continuing to work on my heart, filling it with increasing love. Thank You, Father, for teaching me how to love, embracing change with confidence, and trusting You all the days of my life.

In Jesus' name,
Amen!

YOUR REFLECTIONS

1. Ask God to bring to your mind anyone you need to forgive and write their names here.

2. Write a short prayer forgiving each person who has hurt or harmed you, using additional paper as needed.

THE COMING KING

Last October, my husband and I drove up to Kerrville, Texas, to visit The Coming King Sculpture Prayer Garden. This holy ground is where donor artists have provided fourteen massive bronze sculptures to encourage us to pray for healing, deliverance and signs and wonders.

When we parked our car, our eyes gazed upon the thousand-pound, life-sized Lion of Judah overlooking the Texas Hill country. As we entered the strategically unique twenty-four and a half acre garden, we were welcomed with a sculpture of Jesus holding out a casting net, inviting us to be the fisher of men.

Then, my eyes darted to a man wearing a crown. He was riding a beautiful white horse. I had caught a glimpse of The Coming King.

As we continued to walk to each of the four corners of the cross, my legs became heavy, and I began to ease into worship. By the time I came upon The Divine Servant at the top of the hill, eye level with the horizon, tears began to run down my face. This ultimate representation of humility depicted Jesus washing Simon Peter's feet the night before His crucifixion.

There was something sacredly intimate about worshiping and interceding in between these sculptures. Somewhere between the seventy-seven scripture tiles and God's Rock Garden, I found myself weeping toward The Empty Cross, the seventy-ton reminder that I was bought with a significant price.

As the steel cross towered over me, all doubt was obliterated, and I found myself gazing from the bottom of the cross up to the heavens and remembered the words from Luke 2:8-14, *"in the Highest..."* Never had this seemed more true.

A friend reminded me of something significant. Sometimes it is easier to believe this verse, *"in the highest,"* and yet He is also there in the lowest. Similar to the rolling hills in the Texas Hill country, let us rejoice when we are on the top of the mountain, and let us also be joyful while at the bottom of the valley.

As we prepare for the anticipated season of the coming King, whether it brings heartache, grief, or anxiety, be reminded of the fact that peace and goodwill come to those who are favored.

A Closing Prayer

Heavenly Father,

Thank You for being with me always. While I might not always see You in the midst, let me never forget You are the Coming King. I ask the Holy Spirit to begin directing my steps and let my every move come from You. Lord, if I begin to sway too far left or too far right, I ask You to redirect me in the way You want me to go.

In Jesus' name,
Amen!

YOUR REFLECTIONS

1. Write down 3 things that cause you to rejoice.

2. Write a prayer for a future visit to the valley. For example:
   I am thankful for the times when You ...
   I am reminded that You never left me when ...

PART 2

WILD ROOTS

SURRENDERED HEARTS

How many times did our parents tell us not to touch a hot plate? And what was the first thing some of us did? We touched the plate and burned ourselves. Most of us can agree that our parents seemed to always be nagging us about something. Now, as adults, we realize it was all for our own good; we just could not see it at the time.

Things were not much different two thousand years ago. We read in the book of Judges how the children of Israel did evil in the sight of the Lord, not behind God's back, but blatantly in front of Him, even serving multiple gods of weather, finance, love, and sex.

After years of this blatant idolatry, God was angered enough that He turned the Israelites over to the Philistines and the people of Ammon. We know this broke God's heart, but by allowing them to be conquered and serve other gods, He was giving them what they desired.

Like injured and desperate children, the Israelites cried out to God after constantly being harassed and oppressed. The Scriptures, however, state that despite the fact the children of Israel cried out to the Lord, God said He would not deliver them. This would be the first time it was recorded that God would not save His children. His rejection of the Israelites begs the question: what was lacking in their initial repentance? It was not their voice, but their hearts.

It is one thing to say something, and it is another to put it into action with a surrendered heart. After the people rid themselves of false gods and demonstrated true repentance, God's heart was moved with compassion by their change of heart. His heart could no longer endure the misery of Israel.

Like many loving parents, it is difficult for God to see His children in misery, but He knows we must humble ourselves because it is good for us. Our unfailing and unchanging God still wants our fullest attention and our whole hearts. You can be confident that just as our parents disciplined us for our own good, our God knows what is best, not only for us, but also for His Kingdom.

A CLOSING PRAYER

Lord God,

Take out our stony hearts and put in hearts of flesh so we may feel and love like You do. Let us surrender to You all our burdens and fears. God, forgive us of our idolatrous nature, and remind us of who we belong to. Let us not stray, but instead, fall into Your loving, merciful arms.

In Jesus' name we pray,
Amen!

YOUR REFLECTIONS

1. Write down things you may be putting before God. For example, social media, compulsive shopping, etc.

2. Ask the Lord for forgiveness and then release these things into His hands.

WHAT ON EARTH IS A TRIBE?

"How's your life working for the people around you?" This question was offered to me as a conversation starter, and before I could belt out anything ridiculous, a couple of ladies ran across my mind.

This question came conveniently, just as I had just hung up the phone with, not one, not two, but three of my closest girlfriends. Please understand, I do not use the word *girlfriends* lightly. If you were to ask me three years ago if I had a *tribe*, I would offer up my DNA results from Ancestry.com and say, "Yes, Choctaw." But this is not how the term is used these days.

Tribe is now being used to describe a group of friends who become more like family. This group of friends stick with one another through thick and thin, in good times and in bad. These people, who come together as your tribe, confidently trust you and you trust them.

When the question, "How was my life working for the people around me?" came up, my mind instantly triggered thoughts of the ladies named Kayla and Lana. These were two of the three ladies I had just had long conversations with, and I could not help but ask myself, "I wonder how my life is working for them."

To be completely honest, our friendship is different from others. I embarrassingly researched social media's idea of what *friendship* is supposed to look like, and unfortunately for social media, my friendships do not look like the ones portrayed.

Their friendships toward me, and vice versa, are quite similar. The three of us do not require the attention social media portrays. We can go a week or two, even a month without speaking to one another. Then one of us will contact another, and we pick up right where we left off. We purchase silly gifts for one another, and we tag one another on ridiculously funny inside jokes. Most importantly, we can pick up the phone at any given time, on any given day, and we know, without any doubt, the other will answer.

This was not a prearranged discussion we had with one another, it was not a pinky promise or part of a friendship contract; it just is. And, for a split second, when the question arose, I responded to myself, "I don't know if I'm being a good friend or not." This thought crept in because I was thumbing through social media accounts, looking at wine glasses being raised, selfies of beautiful girls surrounded by balloons and confetti, and all I could think about was that Lana and Kayla were probably in their jammies watching Netflix like I was.

For a moment, I let doubt set in. I saw with my earthly eyes what I *thought* a friendship was supposed to look like. I began to ponder why my "girlfriends" were not blowing kisses at the camera with glitter on our faces. Then Jesus came across my mind and reality set in.

If I remember correctly, Jesus had a tribe. His writings about His tribe did not include happy hour, daily phone calls, and mandatory meet-ups. His tribe wanted to be around because He loved them. Nowhere does it say they were complaining about Jesus, taking selfies, or having brunch. Instead, they came together, broke bread, and gently spoke to one another with the little time they had. They loved one another.

Jesus was there in time of need. He was present when someone needed encouragement or a nice kick in the butt. He listened to their heartaches and pain. He was a Friend.

Our lives are being wrapped up in a rushed routine, when instead, we should be basking in the love each one gives, no matter when or where. It does not have to be every Friday after work. It may be when one of you is not the best version of yourself and the other person helps you, encourages you, loving you through that challenging time.

Friendship is not about the cutest Instagram filter or the greatest number of Likes. Friendship is about love! This love takes sacrifice and commitment. This sacrifice might come at midnight, when everything seems to come crumbling down. This commitment might require you to move some things around in your schedule. Being present for your friends is exactly what we should be doing.

Today I encourage your tribe, girlfriends, or whatever title you want to put on yourselves, to put down your phones and be present at your next coffee date. And here is a biggie: do not take one single photo while you are there. (This is a huge deal coming from a photographer.)

Listen to one another. Put down your calendar, remove your earbuds, and close your laptop. Even if you have to go somewhere new, where it is quaint and there is not so much noise, actively listen to what the other has to say.

Slow down.

Enjoy your time with one another. Rejoice in the adventure. Focus on making memories, not Instagram stories.

Our friendships are more valuable than you can ever imagine. This little group of friends which has turned into family was not designed by your hands. These friends you now call family are a gift to you from God, just as you are to them. Today, I encourage everyone to love harder than you ever have before. One of these days, you too will need this kind of love.

A Closing Prayer

Thank You, Father God, for all my family and friends You have put in my life. You have done an amazing job placing every one of them in my path. It has been my honor and pleasure to continue to learn how to love like You. Lord God, I ask that everyone who reads this be encouraged to be present and always be love, even if we do not know what it looks like. I ask for Your mercy and grace while You teach us.

In Jesus' name,
Amen!

YOUR REFLECTIONS

1. Write down the names of those closest to you. Then, pray for each of them.

2. Handwrite a short letter to each of these people and mail or deliver it to them as a surprise.

HONORING THE SABBATH

A few years ago, during our annual summer vacation, the Lord spoke to me and asked me a very peculiar question. His gentle voice said, "Are you keeping ALL my commandments?"

The short version was no, I was not keeping all His commandments, and the one overlooked was lucky number four:

Remember the Sabbath day, to keep it holy. Six days you shall labor and do all your work, but the seventh day is the Sabbath of the LORD your God. In it you shall do no work: you, nor your son, nor your daughter, nor your male servant, nor your female servant, nor your cattle, nor your stranger who is within your gates. For in six days the LORD made the heavens and the earth, the sea, and all that is in them, and rested the seventh day. Therefore, the LORD blessed the Sabbath day and hallowed it.

Exodus 20:8-11

Late Friday afternoon, my husband and I grabbed our shopping list and headed to our local HEB (grocery store). Funny enough, a slight disagreement tried to rear its ugly head before entering the store, but we clearly knew what it was all about.

The night before we decided to honor our first Sabbath even though we did not have a clue what to do. After shutting down this ridiculous attempt at disagreement, we filled our cart with several goodies, such as manchego, brie and port cheeses, fresh vegetables, and guacamole, and a variety of all things delicious.

As husband and wife, we agreed to turn off all technology for twelve hours. We also decided to cook and bake together, play games, read the Bible, and most importantly, enjoy God's presence throughout the evening.

Three hours in, we started looking awkwardly at each other and asking, "Now what do we do?" We pulled out the game of chess and one of our favorites, Sequence, and the time whizzed by.

We ended the evening with reading the latter part of the book of Jeremiah. We enjoyed the evening as a loving couple and went to sleep before 10:30 PM, knowing by the time we woke up the next morning, our first Sabbath would be in the books, and we were proud.

When 10 AM rolled around, we were bright-eyed and bushy tailed (including our dog, Moose). Dan and I agreed to keep the Sabbath going, so we got dressed, enjoyed a delightful breakfast, and ended our Sabbath with a delicious latte with God.

When I glanced at my watch, it was noon. We had made it eighteen hours without a hint of technology. There was almost zero crying involved, and so much was learned. We were energized, reconnected, and most of all, rested. We could not understand why we had not participated in this commandment before. Even though we had no idea what to do, we had a blast doing it in the presence of God.

I challenge everyone to take a step back and slow down at least one day this week. Turn off all your devices and graciously accept God's gift of rest.

A CLOSING PRAYER

Heavenly Father,

Thank You for all the wonderful things You have blessed me with this year. Your continued outpouring of love is written all over my heart. I thank You, Father, for an exceeding amount of favor and grace. Thank You for a loving spouse, a roof over our heads, and food in our bellies. Thank You for the smallest things, such as a time to read at night and hot tea. Thank You for Your financial provision and for your wild heart, which chases after mine. Thank You for never giving up on me when I stray. Thank You for teaching me how to have a heart like Yours and a willingness to be modified. Thank You, Lord God, for Your consistency, and most of all, Your love.

In Jesus' name,
Amen!

YOUR REFLECTIONS

1. What are your favorite ways to spend time with the Lord?

2. Think of something you could remove from your list of things to do in order to spend more time with God.

BECOMING LOVE

As an extreme extrovert, making friends has never been difficult for me. My childhood best friend, Angela, and I agreed on almost everything. Our personalities differed, but we respected each other's traits. Even when she went to a different high school, our friendship was seamless, strong, and took minimal effort.

Sometime after high school, Angela moved, and things changed. I noticed my new friends were typically male. Although this did not bother me, the girlfriends of those male friends began to have differing opinions. I was completely naive and this all happened unbeknownst to me. I went on with my business as they carried on with their gossip. I decided then to make a vow to not have any other female friends in the future. The stale taste of jealousy, gossip, and anger lingered longer than I expected.

Walls went up with immense pleasure. Why? Because if I did not let anyone in, they could not hurt me.

Then the "I-do-not-care" attitude set in, of course, with walls. I, too, began to hurt other women along the way, not maliciously, but with an undiscovered shiver of regret.

Years went by, and I befriended a confident and sassy woman named Jennifer. Now, Jennifer was the exception, not the rule. She carried herself with humility and enjoyed her introverted space. I did not. I poked and prodded her until she was forced to befriend me as well. We began dancing together on a salsa team, and we have been friends ever since. We had a silent mutual agreement: Do not do anything hurtful to me, and I will not do anything hurtful to you.

Our friendship was excellent. After many years, I had found a woman worth having around, and I did not have to worry about snarly comments, painful regrets, and emotional breakdowns. Four years passed and I slowly let my guard down, all by the grace and love of God.

Slowly God began placing more females in my path. I knew this was God because I had thoroughly enjoyed my drama-free lifestyle. God sent two beautifully vibrant women along my path, women who could not be overlooked. With great hesitation, I began letting Him work on my heart, knowing He wanted to destroy my hardened heart. And He did!

Within three months, both of those women had calloused my heart. My first reaction was to put the walls back up, but to my surprise, the walls were nowhere to be found, only tears. I began inquiring God, wondering what had happened to the "tough girl" and why this hurt so much.

He whispered to me, "Read Colossians 3:12-13." After the tears subsided, I instantly began praying for each of those women. Although the pain did not instantly disappear, within weeks, both of these women came to me with heavy hearts. Conversations were had (apologies were the least of our concern), hugs were exchanged and a few tears were shed. Overall, God had not only created a new heart in me; He have given my new girlfriends new hearts as well. All it took was for me to get out of God's way so He could work on my heart.

Friendships like I have with Angela, Lana, Kayla and Jennifer, that require little or no effort, are rare. This is not the case with most friendships or relationships. Most of our friends have very differing personalities, and God requires us to exert more than the bare minimum of effort to maintain them. Our loving Father requires our hearts to be filled with an unlimited amount of mercy and grace. And, fortunately He is there when things become increasingly uncomfortable.

Build relationships with other people, even if it takes getting out of your comfort zone. Our vulnerability with others will help us to grow and become love.

A CLOSING PRAYER

Father God,

Thank You for continuing to work on my heart, creating a heart as beautiful as Yours. Thank You for being a faithful God, loyal and true. Forgive me, Father, if I have come against You or anyone with an unclean heart. I come with an open heart to accept any changes needed to make me a person worth calling a friend.

In Jesus' name,
Amen!

1. In what ways are you known for your love?

2. Think of someone who has hurt or wronged you in the past. Have you forgiven them? If not, pray and forgive them. If you have wronged someone, call them and ask for forgiveness.

Rose-Colored Glasses

After many months, it was a peaceful, quiet Saturday in our home. It was perfect! My husband and I woke up late. We convinced our dog, Moose, we were asleep by keeping our eyes closed, but both Daniel and I knew the other was awake. We snuggled and enjoyed the sunlight peeking through our bedroom window. It was a whopping 9 o'clock A.M. when we finally rolled out of bed.

Almost instantly we received a group text stating, "Are you guys up yet?" And, for the first time in an exceptionally long time, we had the chance to ignore the text or reply without conviction. It was completely up to us.

We also had the chance to decide whether to go to brunch together or with friends. We take brunch very seriously in the Jackson household.

We responded to the text and met up with a mutual friend at one of our favorite coffee shops. After the normal chit-chat, we sensed our friend had something bothering him. He said, "You know, I am okay at being a graphic designer, and I am okay at playing guitar, but I am not 'great' in any one area, and I do not really know what I am doing. I just want to be good at one or two things."

He turned to me and said, "You are a great at photographer, and you are a great writer." He turned to Daniel and said, "And you're great at technology and a great husband."

I physically shook my head while trying to make sense of why our friend could only see that he was "okay" at the list of traits he had just spilled out. But when he started talking about our qualities, he used the word "great" instead of "okay."

Dan chirped in and reminded our friend that being a "jack of all trades" was a positive attribute. In agreement, I followed up with the fact that having a well-rounded personality has its benefits. You can talk to anyone. And that comes in handy when trying to do what God requires of us all, *make disciples*. What better way to make disciples than to have a personality that can adapt to just about anyone?

In the midst of this conversation, God said to me: "It's only a matter of perspective." We knew the attributes our friend inherited were gifts and callings, things we did not have ourselves, and so we found them fascinating. We believed his qualities made him very well-rounded, communicative, quirky, and funny, but he saw them as mediocrity.

Interestingly enough, the very next day I had a run-in with a different individual who was saying the very same things. This person, whom one would think had everything, felt unfulfilled, unproductive, bored, and frustrated, simply because he did not know his purpose.

I was baffled. I could not fathom the idea of this person, who had a great career, had a lovely home, and owned a new care, was pouring out his heart because he felt completely defeated.

Later that evening, I asked God what this was all about. The Holy Spirit reminded me of something that had happened to me about six months before.

I had been in bed after slamming the phone down because I was filled with frustration. I was on Instagram, scrolling through what seemed like hundreds of local photographers and all their beautiful portfolios. This made me feel so inadequate. Unfortunately, I was scrolling through social media because I had been annoyed with an event earlier in the day that caused me to consider abandoning my blog. I was discouraged because I was not bringing in as many readers as some of my fellow bloggers. I huffed and said, "Why am I even wasting my time?" Then I went to bed, frazzled and annoyed.

When I woke up the next morning, the first thing God told me was, "Stay off social media if you are going to covet others. In fact, look up John 15:16 while you are at it."

I thumbed through my Bible and found the reference. It said, *"You did not choose me, but I chose you and appointed you so that you might go and bear fruit – fruit that will last ..."* Not fame, fruit! Not fortune, fruit! Not Instagram followers, fruit! I knew right then what I had seen on the screen the night before was not what God wanted me to see. The Holy Spirit was reminding me that I, too, had been deceived and felt deflated and unhappy.

What we may think of as a mundane job, personality trait, hobby, or craft, other people who do not have that quality think of as a phenomenal trait or gift. Why is this? Because comparison is the stealer of joy!

What we saw in our friend was through God's eyes and not the rose-colored glasses that he was looking through. He saw only mediocrity, while we saw what Christ sees in our friend. While we saw a perfect home life, a nice career, and a new car, that man saw lack. In his eyes, it was not enough, just as I had seen myself a few months before.

Our friend's discouragement soon passed because he realized it was just a matter of perspective. We must remove the rose-colored glasses we use to hide the truth and see what God sees in us, not what the world puts in our bank accounts, the number of people in the pews, or the number of subscribers to our blog. The ministries we each have may seem insignificant, boring, or mundane, but God has put us in these positions to make disciples, encourage one another, and love as many people as we can. Where we see "Woe is me," God sees it as, "Whoa, it is Me!" It is only a matter of perspective.

We can all see ourselves through the eyes God has given us. At times, we may feel discouraged or like we are fighting a battle alone. This is a lie. God is with you, and He sees you!

As mentioned before, I found myself slightly doubting the words my friend spoke over me that momentous Saturday a few months back. Honestly, I find myself second-guessing myself on a regular basis, looking over other photographer's work and portfolios, wondering how they got there. I read other people's blogs, wishing my own blog would touch the world in the same numbers. And Paul reminds us: this is not what we should set our eyes on, these earthly things.

Joyce Meyers shared a wonderful quote in her Amplified Bible, and it says, "Many believers want the good life, but they passively sit around wishing for something good to happen. If you genuinely want to live the resurrection life, you must have a backbone and not just a wishbone!" That is my girl, Joyce!

So, if I want to be a more successful photographer, then I need to photograph more, advertise more, make my business cards rain like they are hundred-dollar bills.

If I want to be a successful writer, I need to market my blog, go to writing conferences, or take courses. In the infamous words of the Jackson household, "Whatever it takes, make it happen." But we cannot just go around with the rose-colored glasses and expect to see what God sees. We must see and know the truth. We must lift the veil and see past the distorted worldly view.

Romans 8:28 says, *"And we know that all things work together for good to those who love God, to those who are the called according to His purpose."* So, I have a couple of questions:

1. Do you love God?
2. Do you believe you are called for His purpose?

If you answered yes, then you believe the truth, and if this scripture in the Bible is true, then all of it is true.

God did not create us for mediocrity or out of boredom. If we trust confidently in Him, He can take our routine and turn it into righteousness, but we must make sure we do our part and that is to believe in Him.

Of course, God always gives us an option. He gave us free will. We can believe the lies the world has told us about only being "okay" at a handful of things, or we can believe God's Word when it says that we are heirs of the Most High God.

The enemy will do anything in his power to get us to say to ourselves, "Woe is me!" He tries to deceive us into thinking we are unhappy about our situation, but those thoughts are from the enemy and not the thoughts of Jesus who says, "Whoa, it is Me!"

Now that we have cleared up any foggy lenses, we are able to see ourselves the way God sees us and not believe the deception the enemy is spewing at us. In fact, God warns us about this. It is imperative to respect this warning. We must not only obtain these new eyes (and ears), but to see (and hear) through them on a consistent basis, so that we are not deceived.

We are not fighting against flesh and blood but against demonic powers and principalities. Beth Moore says, "Most of these things we are fighting against have had a strong hold in our environments for generations. They will not let go easily. Do not stand down. Stand firm."[1]

Open your eyes! See all the beauty, creativity, and technical abilities God has given you. These are not pointless gifts and attributes; these gifts were handmade to reflect your personality so you could go out and make disciples.

It only takes one photo, one product, one design, one song, one apartment lease, one computer code to convince ourselves that we are only "okay" at what we do, say, write or create. This is absolute garbage. It is trash, and we do not accept this in our lives because we are worthy of so much more.

Take your thoughts captive. God is making it clear that we should heed His warnings and live our lives with the eyes and ears of Christ. When the enemy tries to come in and steal, kill, and

1. Her tweet of April 2, 2019.

destroy, be ready for him. Stand tall and be prepared for warfare. The Gospel is your weapon against all worldly things.

If you believe you have a wonderful idea, be bold and step up. If you are bored, then read, take a continuing education class, create something from nothing. We use a mere ten percent of our brains. Can you imagine what God could do with us if we even put in another five percent of willingness, boldness, and confidence?

Yes, our jobs and lives can be mundane. Yes, we might be overlooked for a higher position. Yes, you might be years overdue for a raise. Yes, you might feel like you deserve a better car, but this does *not* mean you do not have a purpose. This does not mean you are unworthy. This means it is time to embark on a new adventure with God.

Remove those worldly rose-colored glasses that distort the truth and put on the full armor of God. Then, come boldly before the throne with fresh eyes, and make it happen.

A Closing Prayer

Thank you, Lord God, for removing the veil from my eyes so I can see and witness all Your goodness. Let me not be confused by what the world is telling me. Let me not be deceived or misinformed. Deliver me from all unworthiness and teach me to use my gifts and callings to glorify Your name. Amen.

YOUR REFLECTIONS

1. Name 3 great qualities you have.

2. How could you use these qualities to build God's Kingdom?

LOVINGLY NAMED

Falling in love is often described as a feeling of euphoria with an entertaining sense of exhilaration and confusion all at the same time. We are swooped up into another individual's life, and we want nothing more than to spend every waking moment with them. Loneliness and emptiness give way to affection and adoration. Passionate glances and charming pet names like "baby" and "sweetheart" make us blush.

The Lord's delight in us is so much more triumphant than our human pleasures. Christ's love is immeasurable and unfathomable. He takes intense pleasure in His Beloved, and He calls us by a new name.

Our joy cannot be contained when we relish God's love for us. Our jubilant responses include knees buckling in worship, tear-filled eyes, singing praises to His name, and hearts filled with rapturous, unconditional love. This is a love many do not ever encounter.

Unlike human love, which diminishes when we fall into sin, our God declares us His Beloved and patiently "woos" us back. Oh, what great love He lavishes upon us!

Since the beginning of time, God stated that He would not be still or rest until glory, righteousness, and salvation were established in Israel. Our Lord promised to continue working on Israel's restoration, despite their sinful ways. He did not give up on them; nor will He give up on us now.

Israel's land, which was once described as "forsaken and deserted," God christened as "My Delight is in Her" and "Your Land Married." These new alluring names, Beulah and Hephzibah, were bestowed upon Zion as a bridegroom would speak to his bride on their wedding night.

Unlike the romantic love we have here on earth, God's raw and tender *agape* love creates a longing within us to hear those names fall from His lips. No pet name will ever compare to the desirous names given to us by God.

Our loyal, generous God pulls back the veil of His Bride and rejoices tenderly as a newly-wedded husband would do.

Our God is faithful, even when we are not. He restores even when we rebel. Day after day, He delights in you, and He delights in me.

God brought us all out of a desolate place, rescuing us from death and destruction. So, make yourself ready and wear your finest and brightest linens, for the time of the wedding is near.

A Closing Prayer

Heavenly Father,

Thank You for giving me the privilege of having a better connection with You. Thank You for loving me enough to put it on my heart to fast, pray, and worship. I want to praise Your Name above all names because You deserve it. Thank You, Father, for pursuing me, even when I did not pursue You. Thank You for picking me up off my knees when my flesh gets the best of me. I am eternally grateful for Your constant mercy and grace. Thank You, Father God, for teaching me how to strengthen our relationship and for showing me how important it is to become one with You. Thank You, Father, for loving me, always.

In Jesus' name,
Amen!

1. Look up the word *beloved* and write down your favorite definition(s).

2. Look up the following scriptures and write down what God calls you:
   - 1 Peter 2:9
   - Galatians 3:13
   - Romans 5:17
   - Jeremiah 31:3
   - Isaiah 43:4

Part 3

Wild Freedom

COUNT THE COST

A few years ago, my pastor had us watch the film, *God's Generals*, and one of the quotes by Kathyrn Kuhlman brought me to my knees. She said, "It's going to cost you everything." In that moment, when I heard her speak those words on videotape, I experienced a whirlwind of emotions. The word *cost* itself laid heavy on my heart. So, like any nerd would do, I wrote the word *cost* on a Post-it note and placed it in my Bible.

After the video, half of me was prepared to put all my clothes in a suitcase and say to my husband, "Let's go get everybody saved" (having absolutely no idea where we would go)! The other half of me thought about my cute farmhouse kitchen I had just finished setting up and my remote work position from home. I was torn right down the middle.

I sat there with one foot in the Kingdom and the other in the world. I took out the little Post-it note with the word *cost* on it and started digging into the Bible.

In Mark 10, there is a story of a wealthy ruler who came to meet Jesus. He asked Jesus what he needed to do to inherit enteral life. Although he had kept most of the commandments, Jesus compassionately mentioned to him that he needed to do one more thing: *"One thing you lack: Go your way, sell whatever you have and give to the poor, and you will have treasure in heaven; and come, take up the cross, and follow Me"* (Mark 10:21).

Jesus was very pleased that this rich, young ruler was following the commandments, and it was with joy that He told the man to just let go of this one more little thing. In this way, He showed the man the way to eternal life. He gave him the answer he was looking for.

Unfortunately, the young ruler sorrowfully turned and went away. Why? Because he could not let loose of his vice. He had doubts about what Jesus said, and was not willing to take up his cross and deny himself as Jesus was requesting. The cost was too great for him.

This man saw his properties, his money, his other forms of riches, but he could not see the Kingdom. He lacked faith and feared the possibility of not having enough. Nothing in this life is easy or free. And, if it is, you do not want it.

We tend to cry out to God, "Oh, send me! I will do whatever You want me to do." Then when God says, "Okay," and asks us to give up worldly things, we back off. Maybe it is because we cannot let go of our bondages, our vices. We cannot let go of our binge nights with Netflix. We cannot let go of continuously swiping our credit card. We cannot let go of our "signature coffees." We are truly afraid of the cost, as doubt sets in. We are afraid of what God is going to ask us to give up, and that fear is a blockade to the riches of God!

In Mark 12:41-44, people were putting their offerings into the treasury of the Temple in Jerusalem, Jesus was watching, and He called His disciples to watch too. Some were putting in large amounts. Then, along came a widow and threw in *"two mites"*

(mites were ridiculously small copper coins). Although others were tossing in of their *"abundance"* Jesus marveled at the woman in poverty who put in everything she had.

Can you imagine how Jesus felt when He witnessed this woman's level of faith? She knew, without any doubt, God would provide for her. She wholeheartedly believed. She did not worry or fret, she did not call out, begging from the Lord. She put in *"everything she had,"* and she did it with a joyful heart.

Are we afraid of losing our fancy cars, our shiny new phone, or our snazzy new shoes? Could those things be blocking our view of the Kingdom? Yes, they could, and all too often, they are.

Can any of you tell me when God told you to do something and it cost you nothing? No, because in the entire Bible, God does not change. Our God is faithful. The words of our God do not come back to Him void. They accomplish what He intends.

God does not require us to do something if He has not first equipped us. Will God ask you to go out to a store to pray for someone? Maybe. Will God ask you to give up a Saturday and go do prison ministry? Maybe. Will God ask you to set an alarm and spend time with Him at 5 A.M. in the morning? Maybe. Whatever He asks you, it will cost you.

It will cost your humility. It will cost your time. It will cost that snuggly warm spot in your bed. But it will be worth the cost because God already has a wonderful plan for your life. All you must do is say, "Yes."

Do you know what happens when you say, "Yes"? Your family and friends will become Christ believers. You will see illness and disease healed. Favor will be yours.

Yes, salvation is free, but your faithful walk with God is going to cost you everything because He commands us to deny ourselves and follow Him. Let us not focus on what we *have to give up*. Let us throw in our two mites, focusing on becoming disciples, and I promise you: God will take care of the rest.

A CLOSING PRAYER

Father God,

It says in Your Word that You give wisdom to all those who ask. We are asking for wisdom today. Father, show us the way in which You would like for us to conduct our lives. Lord, if there is anything standing in the way of our riches, we ask You to reveal it and to give us strength while You deliver it from us. With Your mighty hand and steadfast love, Father, we will not doubt.

Thank You, Father, for Your continued mercy and grace while we walk this way. Lord, I ask that You take our hand and steady us along the way. Take away the fears and doubts that come between us and You. Fill us up with Your love and remind us of Your promises.

In Jesus' name,
Amen!

YOUR REFLECTIONS

1. What in your life hinders your relationship with God?

2. Name 3 things you could replace with prayer time. This week, take one thing and replace it with prayer. Next week, add another and so on.

BEING VULNERABLE

When Daniel and I were courting, I was living in an upstairs room above a photography studio. One Wednesday evening after church, as usual, I got out of my car, locked it, and sounded the alarm, walked up to the gate, went into the studio, and turned off the alarm. My dog, Blade, greeted me at the door with his butt wagging every which way. I locked the door behind me and headed for some strawberries I knew I had in the kitchen.

Before I could open the fridge door, I heard a thud at the door, and I saw Blade catapulted against the large wooden door. He was barking like I had not ever heard a dog bark before. Someone was trying to get in, but Blade was making sure it did not happen.

Whoever this man was, he had evidently watched me for days or weeks. He knew about what time I would be back, but he had never had the guts to make it to the door. All we found, after the attempted break-in, were his muddy boot prints outside in the yard. They skid across the driveway when he was frightened by the dog.

I instantly called the police. By the time Dan arrived, the police report had been completed. They reassured me that they would stay there the rest of the night.

Dan's father invited me over to their home, but all I could think of was how this man had tried to break it. It was apparent that he had not just tried to barge into the studio and rob the place; he knew I was there. Although he was not able to get any money or camera equipment, he was able to steal a lot more from me. He robbed me of my security. He robbed me of my trust. He stole my reassurance. He stole my sleep. Most of all, he robbed me of my peace.

This instantly put me in a vulnerable position. I could not sleep for days. The fear of someone watching my every move filled my mind. Within a week, I was moving into another apartment.

Many things rob us of our security, trust, and safety. We hear of child abductions, home invasions, and stolen identities, but I want to step into something even deeper.

After the dust had settled, and an abundance of treats were given and trips to dog parks were taken, I could not help but think how the burglar never made it past the door. There are a couple of reasons, I believe, he could not cross the threshold.

Other than my schedule, he did not do much homework. He had not scoped out the property to know we were an expensive, renowned photography studio. He did not expect my dog Blade to be there, or perhaps the man was just was not allowed in. Period!

I thought long and hard about the amount of prayer dedicated to that land. Dan and I alone prayed for the location for at least six months. My little ten by ten room was not much, but it was under my authority.

When vulnerability presents itself, we have two options, two ways to respond to it.

Option 1: With FEAR

Option 2: With FAITH

I want you to highlight this next part. An acronym for FEAR is:

FALSE **E**VIDENCE **A**PPEARING **R**EAL

The acronym for FAITH is:

FULL **A**SSURANCE **I**N **T**HE **H**EART

We cannot expect God to show us the light at the end of a tunnel, because sometimes He will not. We cannot expect God to let us know what He has for us on the other side of vulnerably because it would completely defeat faith in the first place. God does not owe us anything. He gave us everything we needed at the cross. Just because we live in a world of instant gratification does not mean God has to reveal His provisions for us. Remember, we changed, not God. He has stayed the same loving and faithful God He has always been.

John Mark Comer, in his book entitled, *My Name is Hope,* writes, "God built us to live in transparency and vulnerability, not in hiding."[2] This is so true. We are not made to be hiding in the shadows. We are the light. We are not to be timid and afraid, never having answers to the "what ifs" of life. We must be bold, walking through our vulnerabilities! And, whether we sink or swim, we can still be able to say we stood on faith, and that will make our heavenly Father proud. He will not let us drown.

2. (Abilene, TX, Graph Publishing: 2011)

I want us to be mindful of those vulnerable opportunities God puts in our paths—divine appointments, inconvenient prayer opportunities, new job opportunities, or whatever the case may be. We have to choose faith over fear. Otherwise, we will be stuck wondering "what if" for the rest of our lives. I do not want to regret it down the road.

God has so many beautiful things for us, but they will not just be placed in our laps. God is not trying to hide the truth from us. He wants our faith in Him to grow each day, and the only way to do that is to get out of the boat, even if it is a little unnerving.

A CLOSING PRAYER

Father God,

I believe but help my unbelief. I command all fear in my life to flee right now in Your mighty name. I speak faith, protection, and security over my life right now. Lord, I ask that You guide my steps everywhere I go. If, at any point, I have taken a wrong turn or have been deceived, Holy Spirit, turn me around and put me back on track.

This I pray in Jesus' name,
Amen!

YOUR REFLECTIONS

1. Write out 3 ways you can be more vulnerable before the Lord and how you can put them into practice.

2. Write on a separate sheet of paper a list of all your fears. When you have finished, crumple the paper, rip it in half, and throw it in the trash where it belongs.

FINDING FREEDOM

Well, it was bound to happen eventually. Although I had not intended to go back, I found myself again within the confines of the Woodman State Jail in Gatesville, Texas. The guard's large gold keys hung from his oversized gray pants. Behind me were twenty-foot metal fences topped with spirals of barbed wire. A line of women in white jumpsuits walked two by two, staring me down from a few yards up.

There were two gates to walk through, one, where I had to leave any belongings, the other where I had to undergo the vulnerable pat-down and the infamous wand over every inch of my body.

The guards did not smile. There were no, "hellos," only, "next" for the girl behind me to move up to be searched.

This was, in fact, not my first time to go to prison, nor do I plan for it to be my last.

There is something special about prison ministry. It is not only a feeling or emotion. To be honest, it is not even about hearing the stories of drug addiction, theft, or murder. It is about engaging the fatherless, the brokenhearted, and the needy. More importantly, it is about the freedom that comes with the spread of the Good News of Salvation, as well as providing help in a time of trouble. Isaiah 61:1-3 teaches me that I have a responsibility, and I cannot and do not take that responsibility lightly.

A few years back, I had the honor of taking eight other women from our church with me (two of us were veterans, seven new) to the Woodman Unit. We had arrived at the church at 4 a.m. that morning, and Pastor Howard had cooked us a delightful breakfast. There were scrambled eggs, turkey sausage, buttery toast, and piping hot potatoes ("home fries," as he calls them).

Then we all jumped into the van and departed for Gatesville at 4:45 a.m. It was three and a half hour drive. Within minutes, some ladies had dozed off to sleep, while others were much too excited.

I knew this feeling all too well. The butterflies whirl around in your stomach because you have absolutely no idea what to expect. Feelings of doubt and spontaneity come rushing in, and at the same time, your heart will not stop thumping. It is an exhilarating experience!

The clock quickly rolled around to 9 a.m., the ladies began to squirm, and nerves were involuntarily making their hands shake and their words stammer. Stomachs began to ache, and headaches suddenly came on, but because of compassion and grace, encouragement flowed out of my mouth.

I said, "There is going to be one girl. Everyone has that one girl. All the mess and the junk you have gone through all your life, all the trouble you have been in and the grieving you have endured, it is going to come full circle. Today a woman will stand before you, and she is going to have your exact same story, word for word. In that moment, the Holy Spirit is going to pour out of your mouth because today you will realize it was not all for nothing. It was for her."

Now it was time. We prayed corporately, our identifications were taking into custody, and the day of redemption officially began.

In total, eighty Christian women converged at the jail that day, all dedicating their Saturday to encourage more than nine hundred women confined in this unit.

We had no real expectations. I knew whatever these ladies had in mind for the day was not what was going to take place. I especially knew the woman who had stayed on my coattails over the last two months would be the first one out of the gate. And, sure enough, she was.

All nine of us went from pod to pod, singing praises, giving words of encouragement to inmates, praying for redemption and healing, and anticipating a touch from God. Every single woman who had experienced doubts and insecurity on the way up to Gatesville prayed her heart out that day. The women who had been in the van were no longer the same women as they stood beside me. Boldness reigned over the girls, compassion flowed from their lips, and seeds were planted into everyone they spoke to.

Of course, the enemy tried to manifest on numerous occasions, but the girls laid hands on three different women, and they were all healed instantly. The funny thing is that these were counselors, not even inmates! The enemy had no place here, and he certainly was not allowed to attack those women. We were on fire for God.

Hugs were given to a multitude of inmates over a period of five hours. We loved on these women, just as we had been instructed to do more than two thousand years ago. Every time we left a pod, inmates raised their hands and begged for us to stay just a while longer. We dried their tears of joy and wiped away the pain. Our time there was running out.

We only had about thirty-five minutes left when we entered the last pod. There was one particular girl there. Her name was Missy. Well, she was born Melissa, but for some time she had been incapable of pronouncing her name, so she decided to shorten it.

Let me back up for a moment, I am getting a little ahead of myself. Upon arrival at this pod, a guard reminded us that we had no more than thirty minutes. We eagerly entered the pod, knowing this would be the last set of inmates we would be able to encourage that day.

For the first twenty-five minutes or so, a few of us were speaking to a young woman who would be released in two weeks. She had been filled with fear and uncertainty, but after a few minutes, she was feeling secure and confident of her release.

Suddenly one of our prayer partners, Denise, motioned for me to come to a table across the pod. I peeked at the clock and saw the thirty minutes we had when we arrived was now down to five. Jumping to my feet, I rushed to meet the woman sitting in front of Denise.

The woman's dirty blonde hair fell to her shoulders. It was straggly and stringy. I instantly noted she was about my age, but you could tell life had not been kind to her.

"This lady needs prayer," our lead coordinator said to me. "They say she has Huntington's disease."

I asked her name. She fiddled with her tongue, thrusting against her gums and stuttered, "Missy ... or Melissa."

"What's wrong with you, Melissa?" I asked.

Slowly, she began gesturing and mouthing, "I can't think, I can't speak right, and I can't walk."

Boldness poured from my mouth, "It's okay, my God can do anything. Let us start from the top."

We instantly began praying, and the Holy Spirit bound up all thinking difficulties, all cloudiness in her mind and brain. We commanded all neurons and dendrites to function normally and correctly in Jesus' name.

Suddenly, she shook her head and then looked up at me. Something had been loosed. She knew it, and so did I.

We were losing time, so we continued.

"Let us go lower now," I said. "In Jesus' name, loose her tongue!"

Then I encouraged her to say, "Thank You, Jesus, for my healing!"

In a low, raspy voice, she whispered, "Thank You, Jesus, for my healing." It was quiet, but it was clear. She said it again, even louder this time: "Thank You, Jesus, for my healing!"

"I am sorry, Missy," I said, "I did not hear you. What did you say?"

"Thank You, Jesus, for my healing!" she exclaimed flawlessly.

In that moment, the crowd in that room went wild. The mouth of every inmate, believer or not, gaped open, and they were now all on their feet.

Our team leader shouted, "Hey, we gotta go." Unfortunately, when the prison guards say it is time to go, we must go. But God had one thing left to do.

I said to Missy, "By the authority of Jesus Christ, I command you to get up and walk!

Then Missy was up and running around in circles. Forget the walking, she was jogging around the room. Several of her fellow inmates were weeping violently and praising Jesus, and there were no speech impediments.

Missy came back to me, and I held her head in my arms as she wept tears of joy. The last thing I remember is feeling someone pulling me away.

Our time was up, and we were being escorted out. I felt tears streaming down my face. I had not gotten to say good-bye to Missy. She was the one God sent me there for that day.

You may ask, "So, what is the big deal? We see people get healed all the time. We know God does miracles." Well, years ago, my mom suffered a major stroke. Her speech was taken, and so was her ability to walk. Needless to say, Missy hit home for me.

What is more amazing is that day in Gatesville more hope was shed than I had ever seen before. Although God called my mom home to Heaven, my level of faith in the gift of healing increased by the thousands in less than five minutes with Missy. I know, without any doubt, God can and will heal all those who are His dear children.

Even if we do not know what will happen, we need to fervently continue to pray because I have seen what my God can do. He showed off a little bit that Saturday, years ago, and He decided to use me as the voice and vessel.

This moment with Missy will never be forgotten. I was reminded we are not called to be in fear or in shackles. We are not prisoners. God does not break promises; He breaks chains! Whether behind bars or not, we were bought with a hefty price, and both you and I are called to be free!

Did you hear that? That, my friend, is the sound of chains breaking.

A CLOSING PRAYER

Lord God,

Set me on fire for You! I speak freedom and deliverance over my life and the lives of my family and friends. Let the devil's evil ways fall to the ground and shrivel up to nothing. I bind up and cast down all evil spirits trying to attach themselves to me or my family. There is no room for bondage in my life or the life of my family.

In Jesus' name,
Amen!

YOUR REFLECTIONS

1. Look up Ephesians 6:14-17. Write down the six pieces of armor and what God's truth says about what they represent.

2. Write out a prayer asking God for new boldness to step into a new level of faith. Reread this prayer out loud and write out what the Holy Spirit reveals to you on how to proceed.

ADVENTURE 15

FAITH OVER FEAR

Over the last two years, we have witnessed fear rearing its ugly head in so many different forms over the Covid-19 Pandemic. Our neighbors all over the world found themselves scavenging stores with empty shelves because of hysteria.

This disease came out of nowhere, killing family and friends, wreaking havoc all over the world. Businesses shut down, careers were put on hold, and we were ordered to stay home until further notice. What seemed impossible, came to pass. So, why shouldn't we succumb to fear, just like many of those in the world? Because we are believers, and we are confident in God's promises. He commands us, *"Fear not!"*

When God repeats Himself, He is trying to get our attention. The *"fear not"* in Isaiah 41 is no exception. This famously repeated command in the Bible is written three hundred and sixty-five times and seems imperative in our current situation.

Shortly after the command, two powerful promises come from our Lord. We need not be afraid, first, because He is our God and, second, because He will help us. We are His chosen people, and He does not take the lives of His children lightly. Unlike the false idols created by man, God does not falter when trials and tribulation arise. On the contrary, He rises up!

When we intentionally choose to have faith over fear, we surrender our will to God's. This heart posture then allows God to be our Provider and Protector. We want to take control of our lives, especially when we are stretched thin, because we think we know what is best. This is a façade or illusion. We do not know what is best. The only One who knows is our God.

In times of distress, we tend to act irrationally out of fear. We act out in our heightened emotions without thinking it all through. It takes one innocuous spark of fear to set a wildfire of nefarious behavior. But we have a choice. We can choose to freak out or fear not. Our intentional choice to have faith over fear will not only break strongholds, but it gives the Lord the authority to make a way where there seems to be no way.

Fear not, child, God is in control!

CLOSING PRAYER

Lord,

I speak to the spirit of fear and tell it to leave me right now in Jesus' name. There is no room for fear in my life or the lives of those I love. I command all fear to leave my mind, my property, and my place of business. I speak healing and restoration in every open hole and ask for Your protection.

In Jesus' name,
Amen!

YOUR REFLECTIONS

1. What has robbed your of security?

2. Think of 3 ways you might overcome this fear.[1]

---

1. NOTE: Trauma and anxiety are real. Do not discount them. Please see a
   professional.

WHEN GOD SAYS GO

I used to have the very special gift of killing plants. No lie! I was really good at it. A few years ago, I would happily go into Lowes and have all kinds of flowers in my hand, knowing good and well it was their last days here on earth. Season after season, I would try to grow things, like mint, cactus, and succulents, but even aloe would die on me. Eventually I gave up.

Of course, this certainly did not have anything to do with me pushing forward and getting things done my way and relying on my wisdom and knowledge of plants. All I knew was growing plants was clearly not for me, and I decided not to ever touch a plant again.

But then, a few years ago, God had a different plan for me. All of a sudden, people began showering me with plants and flowers, completely out of nowhere. I was shocked, and kept my secret safe. I am sure no one wants to give you plants if you reply with, "Thanks, but it'll be dead by next week."

Shortly thereafter, the owner of the property where we lived came over and said, "If I buy you some roses, would you plant them? All you have to do is follow the instructions on the pot, and they will do great."

I smiled and nodded, and when they arrived, they were all in separate little planters, all cute with their red and pink petals. I silently apologized to them for their presumed death. But I read the instructions and did exactly what they said—nothing more and nothing less, and they survived.

Soon, a good friend of ours who worked at our favorite restaurant said his mint was taking over his garden and he wanted to bless us with some, since I use every ounce of mint they have while we are at his restaurant. He told me, "Carefully scrape off the outer lining of the stems, until you see a fresh, green stem. Then, place them into some water for a week or two, and the roots will begin to grow. After that, just put them in a pot and watch them take over."

I know I had the kid-in-a-candy-store look on my face when he brought them into the restaurant the next day. That afternoon, I did what I was told, and guess what? Roots came out within a week!

As time went by, more plant blessings were given to me. Our friend Bob announced that he, too, was getting a little bombarded with growth and kindly shared with the congregation some of the most beautiful plants and cacti I had ever seen. Later, I decided to pray over the plants while sticking the little guys in their cute, terra-cotta pots because eventually, I assumed, Bob would ask how they were doing.

Prior to these three blessings, my expectation came from my past experiences, and that was: everything I plant, I kill. It did not matter if other people had different experiences. My past thwarted my expectations automatically.

This time around, I came in with guns blazing (no, I am certain that, too, will kill a plant). I decided to stand on other people's faith to believe these plants would survive and bloom.

My perspective and expectations had to change, and I made it as simple as possible in order not to mess it up. Do what you are told. Period! Put in the soil and watch the stem grow. And, guess what? That is not exactly what happened.

Every, single plant took root and began its own bud, not from the original stem, but growth from the soil and completely different stem. This happened to every single one of them. The plants given to me not only lived, but I witnessed something miraculous—growth from the ground up. And, not only with the plants, but in me, as well.

From this, I realized three important things:
1. My job was to plant the seed in good soil (an action).
2. My job was to water the seed when necessary (another action).
3. Most importantly, when I obey, things will grow.

My job was not to make the plant grow. My job was to "go" or to "take action." I had to go and plant the seeds. I had to go and water them when necessary—no more and no less. I could not control the growth itself. They would have to grow on their own.

Growing is automatically part of the process, but it is not my responsibly. My responsibility is to take action on the given instructions.

When we were young, we did not think about growing. It just happened. In fact, if you were anything like me, my parents could not believe how quickly I could grow out of my shoes.

We may have wished to grow up, but we did not go to sleep at night praying to be taller in the morning. We may have wanted to become strong like Popeye, but we did not wrap a measuring tape around our biceps every night. We just ate the spinach that Mom and Dad put in front of us. We knew that if you ate the leafy spinach, we would grow to be strong. It was automatic. Our responsibility was to be obedient, taking action, doing what we were told.

God will make us flourish automatically. This is what a good dad will do. He helps his children grow. It is cause and effect. If I am obedient, I will flourish.

This is not complicated. We have the choice. Just as I know spinach will make me big and strong. I know if I am obedient to God's Word, I will automatically produce good fruit. This goes for everything in our lives. I cannot say "no" if God says "go."

This is just a small example. Most of our adventures with God are much longer and more in depth than this. In fact, it may be about starting a new career, leaving the old one behind after fifteen years. This is especially important in times of doubt and insecurity. We must do our best not to say "no" because in those moments, it is easy to do.

I get it! It is hard to say "yes" to God when things are a little shaky, but falling into disobedience is far worse. I have found many scriptures on obedience, and although I only have a few to share here, this was a reminder of how serious God is about us abiding in His Word.

John 14:23, for example, says, *"Jesus answered and said to him, 'If anyone loves Me, he will keep My word; and My Father will love him, and We will come to him and make Our home with him.'"* God fully understands when we go through rough patches, but He is a Comforter and, in my experience, He will only ask us to move when He knows we can make it through (even if He must hold us up the whole way).

When God is ready for us to start making waves, He expects us to move. Even if we do not have the strength to make that mountain move, we can at least tell the mountain about our God.

David Platt, renowned pastor and author, once said, "Radical obedience to Christ is not easy. It is not comfort, not health, not wealth, and not prosperity in this world. Radical obedience to Christ risks losing all these things. But in the end, such risk finds its reward in Christ. And he is more than enough for us."[5]

God does not expect us to be perfect; He expects us to surrender to His perfect will. He is not just a good God, but He is especially good at being God. And you know what? This helps me trust when He allows trials to come to my life because it is promised that He uses it all for His good.

Let us not worry about growing into our calling. If we are doing what God tells us to do, we will flourish by default. We do not have to worry about what our next mission will be, where we must go next, we must only listen to the still small voice. He will tell us when it is time.

We must plant seeds, water the soil, and most importantly, we must obey. After that, everything will grow according to His perfect will.

---

5. *Radical: Taking Back Your Faith from the American Dream,* (Colorado Springs, CO. Multnomah: 2010)

A CLOSING PRAYER

Heavenly Father,

Teach me to hear and obey Your still, small voice. Let me be sensitive to Your will because I know it is what is best for me. And if I grow weary, help me understand and remind me that I am not ever alone. If there has been any time in which I have been disobedient, I ask for Your forgiveness right now. Cleanse me from all unrighteousness and teach me how to abide in You.

In Your mighty name,
Amen!

YOUR REFLECTIONS

1. Write down something you have wanted to do but have not attempted out of fear. Ask the Lord to reveal how to make this dream a reality.

2. Find a place outside where you can plant something new, an herb, a rosebush, or some seeds. In the spring, do the planting and then watch the miracle of how this new plant grows.

PART 4

TASTING WILD

Martha, Martha, Martha!

Years ago, I was with my two cousins in the hospital, while they underwent a kidney transplant. The procedure was a beautiful success, but a long haul, not only for them, but also for my entire family. A few days later, I went shopping for Thanksgiving and a church potluck, then I spent hours baking several types of cookies for the family.

Thanksgiving finally rolled around, and we traveled to Wharton, Texas, to enjoy a wonderful Thanksgiving. After a long day, I told my husband we need to pick up a Christmas tree, take out all the decorations, and start shopping for Christmas presents. It was then I noticed a twitch had developed in one of my eyes (more on this later).

Four days later I received a frantic phone call from my sister saying they were taking my mom to the ER because she had fallen out of bed. My husband and I rushed to the ER, where she was recovering, but within a few hours, they were talking about amputating her foot, possibly her whole leg. They had found a diabetic ulcer on her foot they were not happy about.

My heart broke, my mind was a mess, and I was exhausted. The enemy was getting the best of me, not only physically, but mentally as well. I had been invited to be the guest speaker at a nearby church for their Women's Advent Dinner, and the enemy had me convinced I would not have enough time to write a sermon or be able to make it to the event at all. It was in that moment I was reminded I had completely forgotten the reason for the season. Not only had I allowed stress and worry into my peaceful life, but I had also let doubt callously lodge itself in my heart.

I had been running myself into the ground. I was saying "yes" to everything, and I was in a whirlwind of anxiety and stress. Why? Because that is what we do, right? This day and age it is all about "getting things done," "making it happen."

It was time for a serious heart check because we all know worry, doubt, and fretting only hinder the flow of God's wisdom. I realized this sacred time of year had been taken over by emotions, and I desperately needed to slow down and take a deep breath from all the holiday rush.

It was time to rethink and reevaluate. I decided to sit down and have a chat with my heavenly Father. I did not open my Bible or even put on worship music. I just put on some hot water and poured a cup of hot tea for Him and a cup for me. This may sound weird to some, but when I find myself in a challenging time, the best way for me to get clarity is to hang out with my Father.

When I need answers, I make a date with Him. It's just Him and me. During this particular date, He spoke to me in the sweetest, most gentle tone. He said, "Peace, my child!"

That was it. Within minutes, my eye had stopped twitching, and my heart was at peace.

I realized I had completely forgotten about what Thanksgiving meant and what December was all about. It was about our Lord and Savior, Jesus Christ, taking on human flesh for us.

Then the Lord led me to a familiar story in the Bible. In Luke 10, we find the story of Mary and Martha (see verses 38-42). As women, I believe most of us can relate to Martha. Although she was levelheaded and seen in the Scriptures as a caretaker of her family and a woman with a gift of hospitality, she needed the Savior to remind her to be still and choose Him. Does this sound familiar?

Jesus had to remind her (as He did me) that although serving is honorable and good, there was something much more important, and it was sitting at His feet (just as Mary was doing). Martha was so super focused on being a host for the Lord that she missed the most important moment she might ever have experienced.

Jesus, for His part, reminded Martha of her own heart. While she was anxious and busy, she missed beautiful moments alone with Him. Yes, Martha was doing good things, but she was not doing the BEST thing. Jesus had to remind her that Mary had chosen the better thing, sitting at His feet.

We must be mindful to keep our eyes on the Lord, and not just be busy doing things *for* Him. If we neglect the precious moments we could be spending with Him, we miss gaining a closer personal relationship with Him. At the end of the day, Jesus wants our hearts and our worship more than anything else.

This is the key to developing a personal and intimate relationship with our Father God, and when we do it, we begin to realize He is what gets us through all the hectic times. A personal and intimate relationship with a father consists of friendship and fellowship, talking with one another, giggling, and laughing, catching up on things. God wants the same thing. He yearns for your friendship and your fellowship with Him. He wants a personal relationship with you! This means time spent in His presence in worship, prayer, and giving thanks.

Intimate time with God does not have to be repetitive or boring. As I mentioned before, my favorite times spent with God have been over coffee. A coffee date with God may sound odd, but it will do a number on your humility! Try going to your favorite coffee shop and ordering two lattes, when there is only one of you there. Invite God into your daily life and see how things begin changing in your life for the good.

Do you know if God likes cupcakes? Ask Him! Say, "God, do you prefer vanilla or chocolate cupcakes?" Then go out and buy some or make cupcakes with your heavenly Father. This is relationship.

Another favorite thing of mine to do is to write love letters to Jesus. This is the intimacy He yearns for.

Invite Him into your life, talk to Him as much as possible. It does not matter if you are filling up your gas tank, going to the gym, or doing something else. Invite Him to go along. Believe me, this is what He wants from us.

I want to invite you to embark on an adventure to slow down and remember why we have Christmas in the first place. I want you to be reminded that Christmas is a gift in itself. All the presents in the world are worth nothing if it means a life without the presence of God. No amount of Gucci and gold can be compared with His presence.

We must realize we have the honor of decorating the tree, we have been given the grace to sing carols, we have been given the knowledge to make gingerbread houses, we are blessed with the opportunity of writing Christmas cards, and we have been given the finances to buy stamps and mail them out. Why? Because God loves us, and He deserves our love in return.

We sometimes forget the reason we do it all in the first place. It is because we received the most precious gift more than two thousand years ago, and that was Jesus Christ. Join me in this time when it is often hectic, frustrating, and stressful. While the world is telling you to go, go, go, instead, quieten your heart and mind and worship Jesus. More than anything else, let us dedicate the holidays to celebrating His birth, and let us do it with exceeding joy.

A CLOSING PRAYER

Heavenly Father,

I want to respond to Your gentle and loving invitation by preparing my heart to receive even more of the life and love contained in the beautiful gift of God. Let me anticipate this gift of adoration in prayer. Lord, intensify my desire to see and wait, just to seek You and Your extraordinary love. Amen.

YOUR REFLECTIONS

1. Write a love letter to Jesus, telling Him what you love, yearn for, or aspire to be.

One Expensive Tomato

One day I stole something that was not mine and learned a hard lesson in the process.

In the mid-1980s, in Pasadena, Texas, there was a local farmers' market with fresh fruits and vegetables in the front of a busy highway. When you walked in, there was a line of registers, and the smell of brown paper bags flooded your nose. Along the aisles were plump green grapes on the vine, sweet oranges as bright as the sun, and a four-foot cardboard box of pinto beans I stuck my hands into to make music.

This particular Saturday morning was special. I had consistently begged my mom for a nickel because we would be going to the farmers' market, and that's where you could find Super Bubble, the infamous multi-colored wrapping cement block of gum.

Upon arrival at the market, my mouth began salivating because I knew once we were done shopping, I would be able to retrieve my gum from the cheap plastic barrel. Time felt like it slowed down, as we walked through each aisle. Mom would pick up fruits and inhale their fragrances, and she gently pressed on the wheat bread to check for its softness. Then she would open a carton of eggs and inspect them to make sure they were not cracked, before finally placing therm in our cart. It felt like an eternity as the nickel burned a hole in my tattered blue jeans.

Finally, we arrived at the last aisle. My eyes gazed upon yellow, green, and luscious red tomatoes on the vine. I could not help myself. I plucked a cherry tomato, rubbed it on my jeans, and popped it into my mouth. Its sweet, tangy juice hit the sides of my mouth, and some dribbled from my lips. My mother looked back at me and saw me chewing on something. "Carolyn Marie, what are you chewing on?" she asked. Whether I lied or told the truth, I cannot remember, but I do remember her next question: "Did you pay for that?" "No," I said.

After that, she didn't say a word. She continued her shopping and eventually ended up at the cashier, just like normal.

The cashier bagged our groceries, and as we began to wrap up, my mom said to the cashier, "My daughter ate one of your tomatoes, and she needs to pay for it." My mouth dropped open, and I was left utterly speechless. I did not have any money ... except my round, shiny nickel, and it was for my gum. I looked at Mom, and I looked at the cashier.

The cashier tried to convince Mom that it was not a problem, but Mom shot her a look and insisted. In fact, she recommended that the tomato cost "about a nickel." With tears welling up in my eyes, I handed over my precious nickel.

The lesson my mom instilled in me that day was that I could not take what was not mine. It was a tough lesson for a five-year-old, but the message was loud and clear. We cannot rummage through life, picking and choosing things that we want but are not ours to freely take for ourselves. In this life, everything comes at a cost, even if it does not have a monetary value. Some things cost time, and others cost character. We must take these things in consideration. Most things in this life that are free are not worth having.

If my mom had allowed me to eat that tomato without paying for it, who knows where I would have ended up. I may not have grown up to be a thief, ransacking people's homes, but I may have learned to take what was not mine and not feel a bit guilty about it. While, in that moment, I was ashamed and embarrassed, it was a life lesson that was priceless.

Galatians 5:22-23 tell us:

But the fruit of the Spirit is love, joy, peace, longsuffering, kindness, goodness, faithfulness, gentleness, self-control. Against such there is no law.

Love, joy, peace, patience, kindness, goodness, faithfulness, gentleness, and self-control ... most of us know these as the nine fruits of the Spirit. The priceless lesson my mother taught me was imperative for my future spiritual walk with God. Learning not to take what was not mine was just one step toward finding and enjoying the goodness of God. This happened long before I even knew much about Jesus. What I did not know then was that self-discipline and self-control would be a life-long journey.

Whether we struggle with eating too many cookies, chugging down three lattes a day, or snagging a few grapes at the grocery store to "make sure they are ripe," we must do a better job of controlling our fleshly desires. Just because we live in pleasure-seeking, instant gratification culture does not give us a reason to do whatever we want without consequences. While hunger pangs are real, and God given, the Lord did not ever want food to control us. He did not create all of this beauty to control us. He made it to sustain us. His Word declares:

> For this very reason, make every effort to add to your faith goodness; and to goodness, knowledge; and to knowledge, self-control; and to self-control, perseverance; and to perseverance, godliness; and to godliness, mutual affection; and to mutual affection, love.　　　　　2 Peter 1:5-7

Did you see it? One always leads to another. All the fruits of the Spirit lead to the final destination, and that is love. Love will always be the ultimate goal.

Today, I challenge you to begin working on those nine fruits of the Spirit. Although this takes time, obedience, and lots of character building, it will be worth it. Remember, while we have a loving, gentle, kind, and forgiving God, He is still just (see 2 Thessalonians 1:6,) and there will always be consequences to our sin.

God will still correct us when we have stumbled onto the wrong path. He does not look favorably onto sin. He is also omnipresent, so He sees everything, He's not happy about it, and He wants nothing more than for us to turn from our ways and ask for forgiveness.

My goal here is to remind you God is not mad at you, but He might be correcting you. Do not be weary because these two can look very much alike. God said:

> My son, do not despise the chastening of the LORD,
> Nor detest His correction;

For whom the LORD loves He corrects,
Just as a father the son in whom he delights.

Proverbs 3:11-12

If you think God seems to be on vacation or you are not hearing from Him, go back to square one and remember the last thing He told you to do. Did you do it? If not, it's time to repent, move forward, and get back on the footpath He gave you.

A good Father corrects His children, even if it costs us our humility ... or our nickel.

A CLOSING PRAYER

Lord God, sin creeps in, and sometimes it seeps out, but I choose today to repent from my ways. Forgive me, Father, for my gluttonousness ways. Teach me, Lord, self-control and how to stand firm against my fleshly temptations and desires. Guard my heart, my eyes, and my ears from all things not of You, Lord. Help me keep my eyes on You, and let my feet be guided by Your Light.

In Jesus' name,
Amen!

YOUR REFLECTIONS

1. Write down the 9 fruits of the Spirit.

2. Pray and ask God which one you should start working on this month. Next month, ask for another.

WELCOME TO THE TABLE

For about nine years, I was terrified of being around the dinner table. I hated going on double dates or to friends' gatherings because it was usually over a meal. I had stumbled into an eating disorder sometime during college because I had let the enemy have my ear. He would tell me I was fat and ugly, and no one wanted me. Of course, these were all lies because I was always surrounded by family and friends.

In the summer of 2015, Daniel, his Dad, and his sister Coleen and I went on our first road trip together. We found ourselves in Chicago, and wherever we turned, there was a deep-dish pizza. Back then, I was just getting to know God on a deeper level, but more like a New York style "thin crust," not so much deep-dish. After many months of internal prayers, somewhere along the trip, out of nowhere, I was completely delivered from my eating disorder. Literally, poof! Out of nowhere, it was gone!

I will never forget how it happened. We all sat down at Gino's East Pizzeria, and I delighted in the most delicious pizza I had ever tasted. Of course, I did not say anything to any of them because they would have thought I was crazy! I had not told Daniel about my past yet, but here I was, six months into praying, and I could hardly believe I was sitting around the table eating a four-inch-deep pizza.

When we returned to Houston, I began opening up about my past struggles and realized I was not the only one with baggage. A year later, Daniel surprisingly popped the question, and three months after that, we were married. Months flew by, and we adjusted to our new marital routines.

In August 2017, we experienced our first catastrophe—Hurricane Harvey. A large oak tree came crashing down onto our roof. We were extremely fortunate, but this was not the case for many other Houstonians. Over the next couple of days, friends began gathering in our home for food and shelter. At night, we played cards and ate "rainbow spaghetti" that my friend Jenn made (by the way, Dan will not eat my spaghetti unless it is made with colorful noodles,) and for a moment, we forgot that out entire community was under water.

Then, in February of 2021, Houston was hit by a historic winter snowstorm. Water pipes all over the city began to burst, and firewood was impossible to find. The electricity and water were out for days, and we began putting our refrigerated items outside in the snow and filling our bathtub with water. We made peanut butter balls by flashlight, and, on day three, figured out that our fireplace worked. It was a long, cold week for us all, but once again our little piece of heaven kept us safe and warm.

As I recently packed up to move to our new home, I realized that our home, over the last five years, has been filled with friends for Monday Miles (my weekly rides with a Christian cycling team), game nights, worship, and prayer. We had sleepovers with grown men the night before our cycling group, SlowSpokes' first MS150 bike ride. Curled up on the couch, the guys were awakened by the dog, Blade's rumbling, hungry stomach and their toes being licked. Within thirty minutes, the house smelled of freshly scrambled eggs and buttered toast, and everyone prayed around the table for supernatural endurance to ride 180 miles over the next two days.

Over time, more people would come over, some inviting themselves, bringing lounge chairs, bean bags, or coolers to sit on because our table could only seat four. Charcuterie boards, also known as "Adult Lunchables" filled with meats and cheeses, plump bing cherries and mouth-watering dark chocolates covered our countertops and Daniel's infamous guacamole was always emptied first. Some nights we would dine on homemade tacos with pico de gallo and avocado falling out of each end of the tortillas.

During the holidays, Daniel and I would turn up the music and turn on the oven. We would empty the table, wipe, clean, and dry it, only to cover it back up with powdery flour. Because my family could not agree on one type of cookie, we baked them all!

Finally, I realized something spectacular: most of our memories were made around the table. This made me think what the wedding at Cana must have looked like or even the Last Supper. I wondered if it would look like our table. In my spirit, I believe it did.

Rachel Evans says it best, "This is what God's Kingdom is like: a bunch of outcasts and oddballs gathered at a table, not because they are rich or worthy or good, but because they are hungry, because they said yes. And there's always room for more."³ This made me think: What does the Bible say about the table? I read John 12:1-7, and I encourage you to read it too. I encourage you to invite others to your table because this is where miracles happen!

We need to yearn to be more like Lady Wisdom and not be swallowed up by the evil Woman Folly spoken of in Proverbs 9. We must realize it does not matter if all our plates match or how messy our pantry is. It does not matter if we burned the casserole and had to order take-out. What matters is having a relationship with the Lord and with others.

Over the years, we witnessed births and shed tears about death, we told stories, wiped tears, and made new memories along the way. And guess what? They all happened around our table.

Breaking bread, sharing a meal, and being together in fellowship is imperative in today's age because the world is trying to convince us to work harder and faster, leaving no time for our spouse, family, and friends.

Yes, life happens, and sometimes you must eat on the run, but make it a new habit to slow down and share your heart with others around the table. Turn off your cellphones and speak to one another.

Let me remind you: Your table is a sacred space. It has been prepared for you by the Most High God, and He is inviting you to dine with Him. Savor these moments because they will not last forever.

3. Searching for Sundays: Loving, Leaving and Finding the Church (Nashville, TN, Nelson Books:2015).

A CLOSING PRAYER

I want to leave you with a very popular verse found in Psalm 23.

The LORD is my shepherd; I shall not want.
He makes me to lie down in green pastures;
He leads me beside the still waters.
He restores my soul;
He leads me in the paths of righteousness
For His name's sake.
Yea, though I walk through the valley of the shadow of death,
I will fear no evil;
For You are with me;
Your rod and Your staff, they comfort me.
You prepare a table before me in the presence of my enemies;
You anoint my head with oil;
My cup runs over.
Surely goodness and mercy shall follow me
All the days of my life;
And I will dwell in the house of the LORD
Forever.

YOUR REFLECTIONS

1. Go from room to room and pray over your home. For example, "Lord God, thank You for my home. Please protect me and my family from any ... ."

2. Write out 3 to 5 reasons why you are grateful to have your home.

TASTE AND SEE

Not so long ago I was reading a book by Louie Giglio entitled *Don't Give the Enemy a Seat at Your Table.*[4] I was able to share in our church about being delivered from my eating disorder and how, shortly after the miraculous healing, the enemy was right there throwing problems my way. Thankfully, God gave me revelation by showing me most memories were made around the table.

We discussed another big topic, and that is the fact that the enemy wants us to stop gathering, fellowshipping, and making disciples. What can we do to make sure the enemy cannot weasel his way into our lives and disrupt our time with one another? Never invite him in!

If we never invite the devil to dine with us, he cannot come in. If we do not make time or space for him, he will lose ground, not gain it.

This reminds me of Jesus in the Temple in Matthew 21:12-17. He overturned their tables. Why? Because they were mucking up what had been holy and scared ground, and He was not about to let them continue their debauchery.

4. (Nashville, TN., Thomas Nelson Publishing:2012)

How do we make sure we do not give the enemy time or space? We fill our time and space with prayer and thanksgiving.

Please know, I am not telling you to physically turn over tables like Jesus did, but I am encouraging you to do it spiritually. Cast the devil out, and take what is rightfully yours. My table is holy ground, and the enemy is not invited to fellowship there.

How about your table? What are some ways we let the devil dine with us? One of the most commons way we are seeing these days is being too busy.

When I was in middle school, my mom would put a twenty-dollar bill in the middle of the table under the fresh tortillas and say, "Carolyn, if you speak Spanish the entire time during dinner, I will give this money to you." Every day, for God knows how long, I was never able to make it. I was too embarrassed or annoyed by how mom was singling me out. Why did she do that? She knew how important it would be for me to be bilingual.

But guess what? The enemy had my ear! Not once was I able to take the the twenty-dollar bill. The enemy convinced me that my friends would make fun of me if I spoke another language. Now, of course as an adult, I kick myself in the tail because re-learning a natural-born language when you are in your thirties is tough. But I let the devil bend my ear and convince me otherwise.

Around the same time, my entire family would huddle into my grandparent's small house in Galena Park. Every Thanksgiving and Christmas my family would sit around the small table making handmade tamales. One aunt would grind the pork, another would smear the *masa* on the husk, and another would fold and stack the finished product. All the while, my grandmother would be laughing and carrying on around the stove. They always urged me to go into the kitchen and pick up one of the duties, but the *masa* felt gross on my hands, and I preferred to play with my cousins outside.

What these incredible Soto women were trying to do was instill real-life skills with me and share with me their homemade recipes. In this way, they wanted to share life and a love for what was sacred and holy. But I was too busy, too preoccupied with wanting something else, and I missed something monumental to my life – wisdom. The enemy had convinced me that what they were doing was silly and boring, but what was really happening was love brewing around the table.

Invite God to your table and dismiss the devil. We cannot be too busy or rebellious because this is only an invitation to the enemy.

I encourage you to invite the Holy Spirit to dine with you and delight with you in life's everyday joys. Put out your finest plastic ware and plates and ask God, "Would You like water or sweet tea?

Open your table, and invite others to join you in fellowship. Be hungry for hope. Taste and see!

A CLOSING PRAYER

Lord God,

I hunger for You! And I hunger for fellowship with others. Father God, help me to open my heart to invite others to the table. I know it does not matter what my table looks like because it is about the company and not the "mess." You are welcome here, Holy Spirit. Bring to my mind anyone You would like me to invite so that I can minister to them.

Amen!

YOUR REFLECTIONS

1. Ask the Lord to release a divine appointment with someone new.

2. Tonight, over dinner, personally invite the Lord to join you. It can be an intimate or casual event. Light a candle, put out a plate for Him, etc.

SLAY THE LION AND PASS THE HONEY

As I was growing up, my family and I attended a huge Catholic church. After a long mass, we would come home and kick off our Sunday shoes, and mom would pour us each a big glass of sweet tea. It was a mechanical response.

This was not just a Sunday thing. I remember well those scorching summer days when we would get a big, old glass and head out to the pool or hang out on the porch. Everyone had their own glass, and it was how we would spend our days. I was raised on Sweet Tea and Jesus.

When I first met Daniel, we would go out on our dates, and he would order unsweet tea. I would just look at him, bewildered. Then I would tear open my packet of Stevia, place it in my unsweetened tea, and make it taste like how God intended.

Over time, we would begin having dinner with his dad and sister Coleen, who both also drank unsweet tea. Every time they would take a drink, I would gag a little inside. "How can you guys drink your tea like that?" I would ask. Eventually I figured out it was because his dad was from up north and brought down those habits.

Back a few years ago, Stevia was not nearly as popular as it is now. You either chose the pink, the blue or the white packet. Since I am odd, I would carry around some packets of Stevia everywhere we went. On numerous occasions, my friends and family would stare and ask, "Did you bring your own sweetener?"

Proudly I would answer, "YES! Do you need some?" And, on occasion, they would take it.

I did this because, unfortunately, unless you sweeten tea while it's hot and freshly brewed, honey will not melt in it. It will just sink to the bottom of your glass.

In the Bible, we read a lot about the words *sweet* and *honey.* The word *honey* is mentioned sixty-one times in the Bible. It is found in both the Old and the New Testament. This word *honey*, when used in the Bible, usually represents "delight and joy" because of its all-natural sweetness. It can also symbolize "good health, abundance, and prosperity." Honey was known as a delicacy and a luxury. It represented God's provision for His people as a product of the Promised Land. It was, God said, *"a land flowing with milk and honey."*

We find the word *honey* numerous times in the Psalms and in Matthew, Mark, and Luke. But the scripture on which I want to focus our attention today is a peculiar one, found in Judges 14:5-9.

Here we have Samson, who went down to a Philistine city in Canaan. He caught the eye of a young woman there, and then he went back to tell his parents about his newfound love interest. Unfortunately, his parents were less than excited about this woman and asked why he could not find a woman "like them." Eventually, he convinced his father to retrieve her. Unbeknownst to them all, this was all a set-up by the Lord.

Earlier in the narrative, we read Samson went into the vineyards of Timnah and, to his surprise, was greeted by a roaring lion. Then the Spirit of the Lord came mightily upon Him, and he ripped the lion apart as if it were a little goat.

Samson did not have a sword or dagger. He accomplished this with his bare hands.

Eventually he went back and found the carcass of the lion, and there was a swarm of bees living inside it, and they had filled it with honey. He reached in with his hands, grabbed some of that honey, and delighted in it. There was so much honey, by the time he arrived back to his parents, he gave some honey to them as well.

Now here is why I said this is a peculiar story. Samson was able to slay a lion with his bare hands, and they were not harmed. After the lion deteriorated into a carcass, a swarm of bees nested inside, and we do not read of a single bee sting when Samson put his hands into that swarm of bees. He took the honey for him and for his parents in his hands.

Now, let us tackles these one by one. First, Samson killed a lion with his bare hands. When you have a lion coming at you full force (let us call this a sin or conflict in your life), it is frightening. It is loud, thunderous, terrifying and can seem too much to bear. But when you have the Holy Spirit in your corner (as Samson did), you are not fighting alone. The Spirit of God is fighting the conflict, temptation, or sin.

If you are brave enough to stand your ground, God will defeat the enemy and rip him to shreds. He will not be cowering in the corner. He will not be driven away. No, He will tear the lion apart like a young goat. Strength like this can only come from being under the influence of the Holy Spirit.

Remember, the devil is not going to come knocking on your door, giving you a reminder that he will be back next week. This junk comes when we are not prepared for it, like it happened with Samson. He was not out hunting for a meal; he was daydreaming about some cute girl. But out of nowhere the evil one made his way into his life, and he had the option to fight or take flight.

The Holy Spirit is our Helper when we are in trouble or in need. *"No weapon formed against you shall prosper"* (Isaiah 54:17). Period! And guess what. Samson's hands were not harmed.

Next, Samson put his hands into a swarm of bees. I do not know about you, but growing up in the country, I have had my fair share of dead carcasses. Whether it was deer, cows, pigs, you name it, I have seen it all, but I never once saw honeybees inside of a dead animal. Flies? Maggots? Yes, but I have never seen a honeycomb inside the rib cage of an animal. I paint this graphic picture for you because I want you to realize this was a miracle.

After some research, I found there are three species of bees that demonstrate this behavior. However, they do not produce a sweet nectar like we read about in Judges. What God showed me was Samson tasted sweet victory, and this produced an exuberant amount of joy.

With good reason. Samson was weaponless and fighting for his life, and God turned it into good. Then, because our God likes to show off a bit, when Samson returned, God gave him a sweet reminder that he was never alone.

What Samson found was not just a little honeycomb, like you find at an overpriced café on your charcuterie board. No, this was heaping mounds of honeycomb, enough for him and for his parents as well.

An even greater miracle is the bees did not sting Samson. His hands did not swell up. Those hands still had work to do. God needed those hands for one more thing, which leads me to my last point.

Samson dived in with both hands and pulled out the delicious honeycombs. They had no Tupperware back then, and yet Samson not only told his parents about the honey; he gave them some from his bare hands. These were the same hands that slew the hellish lion, the hands not stung by a swarm of bees, hands blessed by God.

Can you imagine how sweet the honey was? I imagine Samson walked around with warm, sticky hands, so full of joy. It was so spiritually sweet, he could not resist, and he shared it with his parents.

Who cares if the honey was overflowing from his hands? When sweet, spiritual honey drips all around, it is never in vain. The honey blesses everything it touches and every mouth it feeds.

Do not just talk about your Christian experience. Carry some around with you, pouring sweet nectar onto everyone you meet, especially those who are needy, angry, or just downright sour. Let them eat from it. Bless others with it. Do not be afraid to let your faith overflow from your hands. Everyone who has a taste for God's righteousness, will taste and see that it is good. Glorify God by proclaiming His sweetness.

Now slay that lion, and then reach deep down in the carcass, bury your hands in God's sweet, sweet honey, and share it with everyone you meet along the way. Just slay the lion and pass the honey.

A CLOSING PRAYER

Heavenly Father,

You are my Comforter, my Protector, and my Best Friend. I do not want to do anything without You. I realize now there is nothing I need to be afraid of because You are always with me. Lord God, I am ready to take this journey with you. And, Holy Spirit, you are always welcome here.

In Jesus' name,
Amen!

YOUR REFLECTIONS

1. List down the ways you have been brave.

2. Write down creative ways you want to encounter God.

EPILOGUE

Wild Adventurer,

Thank you for joining me on these grace-filled adventures that have taken place over the last ten years of my life. After numerous years of doing things my way, I finally came to realize God's journey is not only more spontaneous but also more magnificent than I had ever imagined.

It takes courage to let your guard down and walk in God's grace, peace, and love. Instead of being filled with fear and angst, God was able to mend my heart and teach me how to be audacious and humble.

Let us stop focusing on the rear-view mirror of life and find joy in the journey ahead of us. I am challenging you to get lost in the love of God.

ACKNOWLEDGMENTS

This book would have never come into existence if it were not for Jesus. My Savior gave me the courage, strength, perseverance, and audacity to go on an adventure. Lord, thank You for chasing me for all those years and steering me in the right direction.

To Daniel, my best friend: thank you for supporting me in the darkest of hours when I wanted to give up and throw it all away. Thank you for gently pushing me toward my hopes and dreams, even when I did not want to continue. Thank you for not ever saying no to "just one more book." You're the love of my life, always. By the way, tag! You're it.

To my late mother: thank you for letting me fall on my tail because I needed to learn the hard way. Thank you for teaching me how to fish, bake, and to be a good wife. Over the years, you taught me to be independent, wildly creative, and unapologetically inquisitive. You reminded me to always speak the truth, even if it hurts, to be brave, even when I was scared, and to love, whether I felt like it or not. And for this, I am grateful. Thank you for my first dictionary. How did you know?

I come from a blended family, and while it may not be societies first choice, God made it work for us. There was not a time I ever doubted either of my dads' love for me.

Daddy: thank you for teaching me how to tie an arbor knot and spool a fishing line. Thank you for taking me hunting, teaching me how to two-step, and to wear overalls and boots like a real cowboy. Thank you for teaching me to grow chile piquín and tomatoes and to made a delicious pot of frijoles. Thank you for teaching me how to care for horses and for reminding me that money doesn't buy happiness. Thank you for loving me so well.

Dad: thank you for being there—always. Thank you for loving and caring for Mom until her last breath. Thank you for always letting me have a little "jingle" in my pocket. Thank you for showing me how to treat my significant other with love and respect, especially when I didn't want to. Thank you for teaching me how to wrangle cows, drive an F150 at fourteen, and for keeping secrets from Mom when I know you told her. Thank you for loving me as one of your own.

To Alexander and Linda Rogers: thank you for showing me how to take on the world and photograph every moment of it. Thank you for dragging me to Second Baptist Church and instilling in me that God always comes first.

Kayla: Thank you for helping ignite my passion for travel and always supporting my wild nature.

Lana: Thank you for showing me how to get my hands dirty and to create beautiful things with my hands.

Victor, Patty, and Jennifer: thank you for being there when my life was in shambles and as I gave myself over to the Lord. Thank you for holding my hand and being there when I was washed by the water.

To Howard, Our Fellowship Christian Church, and my Bible Study Ladies: thank you for taking a chance on me, even when I did not know I had it in me. Thank you for allowing me to come up and share what God has poured out on my heart. You have given me the opportunity to share my testimony, pray for others, and encourage as many people as possible. Thank you for supporting me and my ministry.

To Shawn Shannon: to the first woman I ever wrote a book for. Okay, maybe it was just a long essay, but you know how I feel about you. Thank you for showing me not to ever be afraid of an empty sheet of paper and for loving me the way you do.

To Sarah Lattimer: Thank you for being such a great "big sister." While I know God has so much more to our story, it has been a blast thus far. Remember, 42 is the answer to everything.

To Carlos Ichter: thank you for teaching me what a true leader and disciple look like. All the times I tried to sneak out, you never let me throw in the towel. Thank you for showing me how to love

God well and how to worship to my fullest capacity. Thank you for teaching me how to write effectively and how to express my words to others. I will forever be grateful for your daunting red pen and the tenacity you have for loving others well.

To Gary Revis, mentor and academia fanatic: thank you for taking me under your wing and pushing me to focus my energy on my God-given talents. Thank you for making me strive for the impossible and reminding me that nothing is out of reach. Thank you for trusting me, guiding me, and showing me academics is not everything, but wisdom is a priceless commodity.

To Baylor University, George W. Truett Theological Seminary, and the Professional Writing and Rhetoric Department: if it were not for Jo Ann Reinowski, Dr. T.J. Geiger, and Lauren Short, this book would not be here. Thank you for substituting my electives, giving me the chance to work alongside other writers. I will be eternally grateful for all the edits, rewrites, and constructive criticism. You have all molded me into what I have always wanted to be, an author.

To John Tillman, Jon Polk, and The Park Forum: you are all so precious to me. Thank you for opening your hearts and encouraging seminarians to write down all of God's good and pleasing work. Proposing, organizing, compiling, and editing amateur writer's devotionals cannot be for the faint of heart, but you follow God's request anyway. Thank you for these opportunities to be a successful writer.

Acknowledgments

To Harold and Andy, the best publisher and his tea-loving wife: You two are absolutely incredible. Thank you for making my dream finally come true. What was a heap of mess for more than a year and a half you have made into a masterpiece. Thank you. I will forever be grateful for all the proofing, edits, re-writes, and late night revisions. Thank you for never giving up on me.

If I were to name and thank every person who has helped me along the way, I would have to write another book. For now, know that Post-it notes, social media posts, encouraging words, and late-night texts do not go unnoticed. Thank you for reminding me to never give up on my wildest dreams.

AUTHOR CONTACT PAGE

You may contact the author directly at:

info@carolynsotojackson.com